MW00905423

This coloring book belongs to:

____

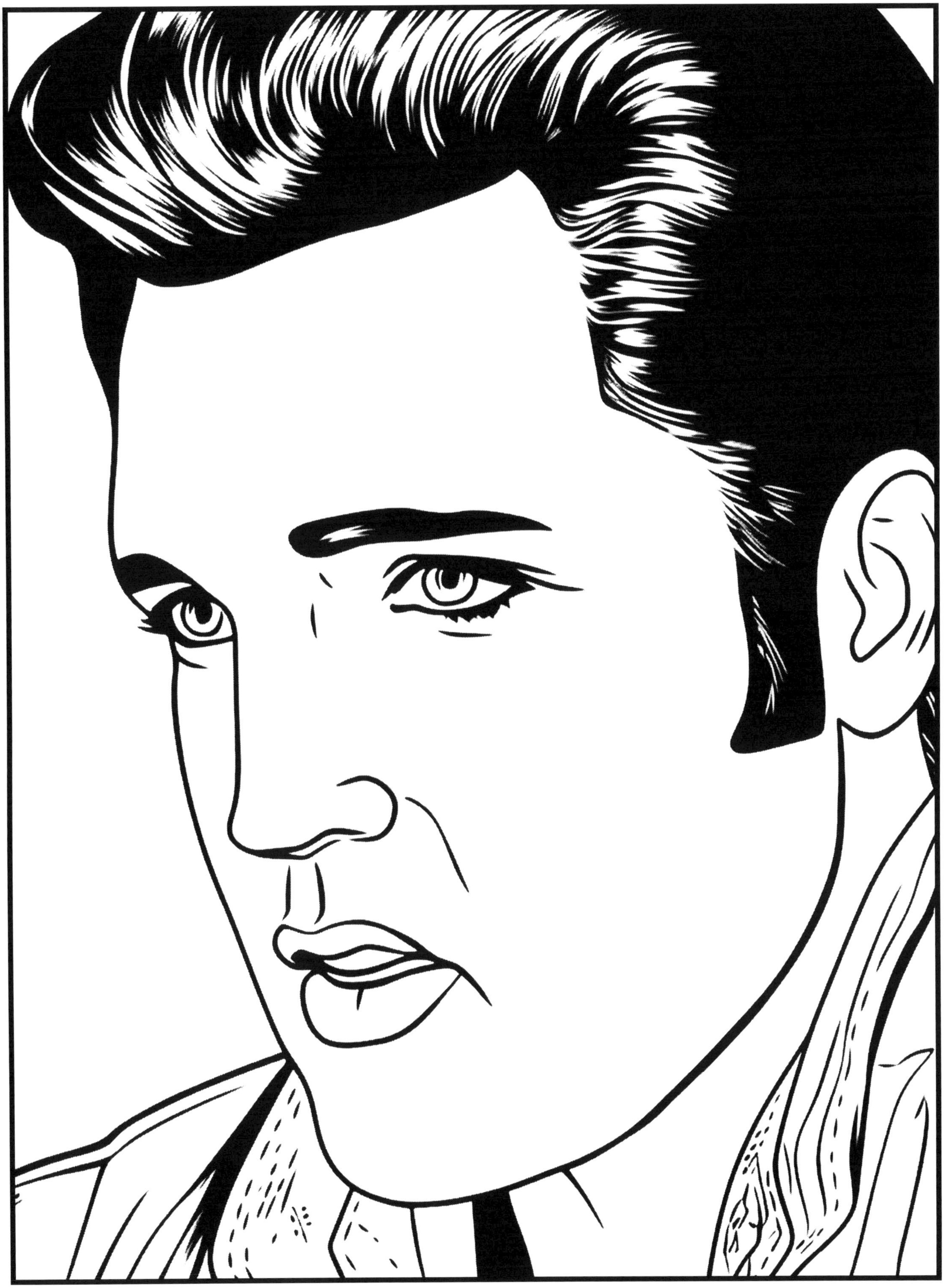

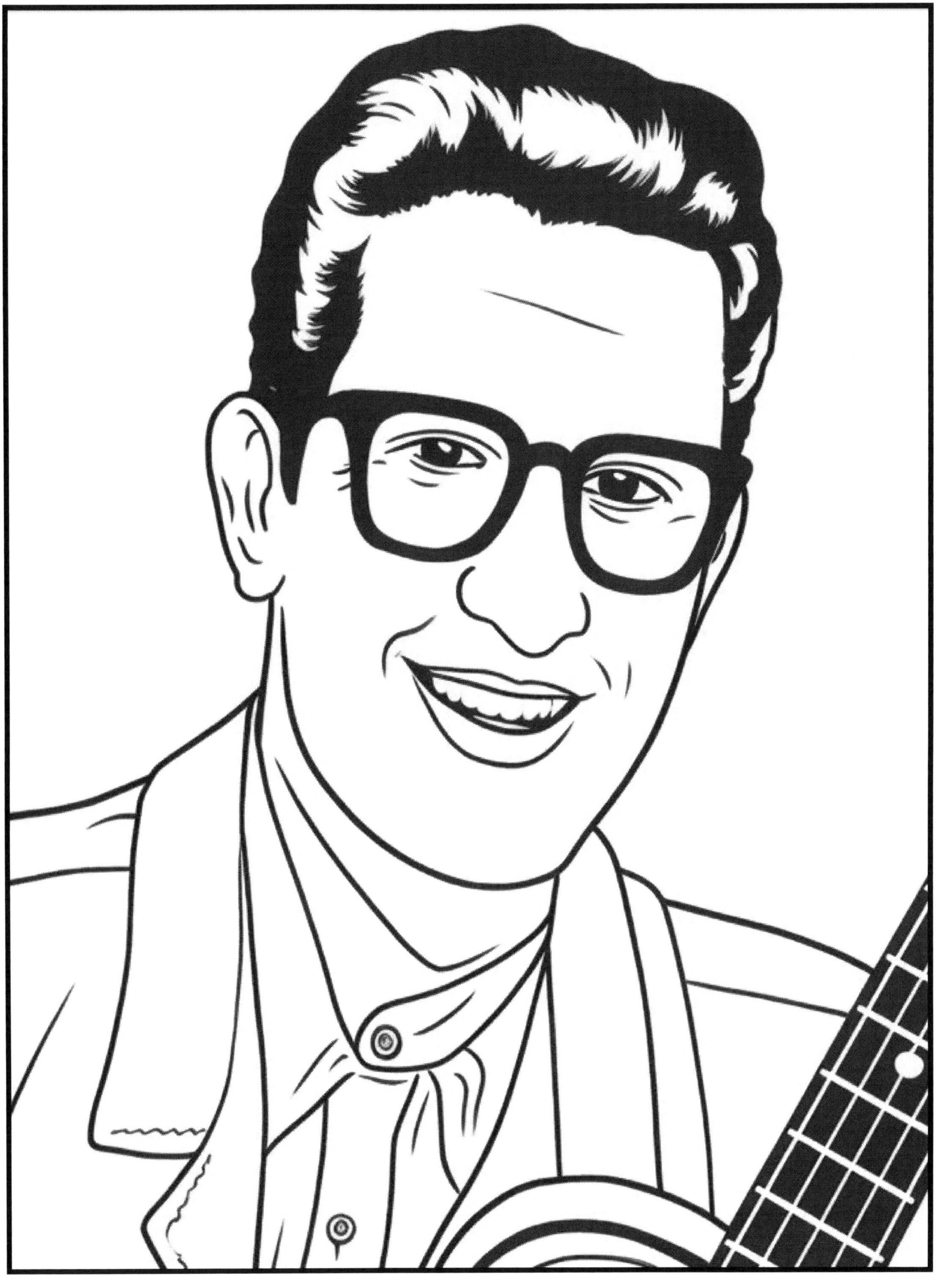

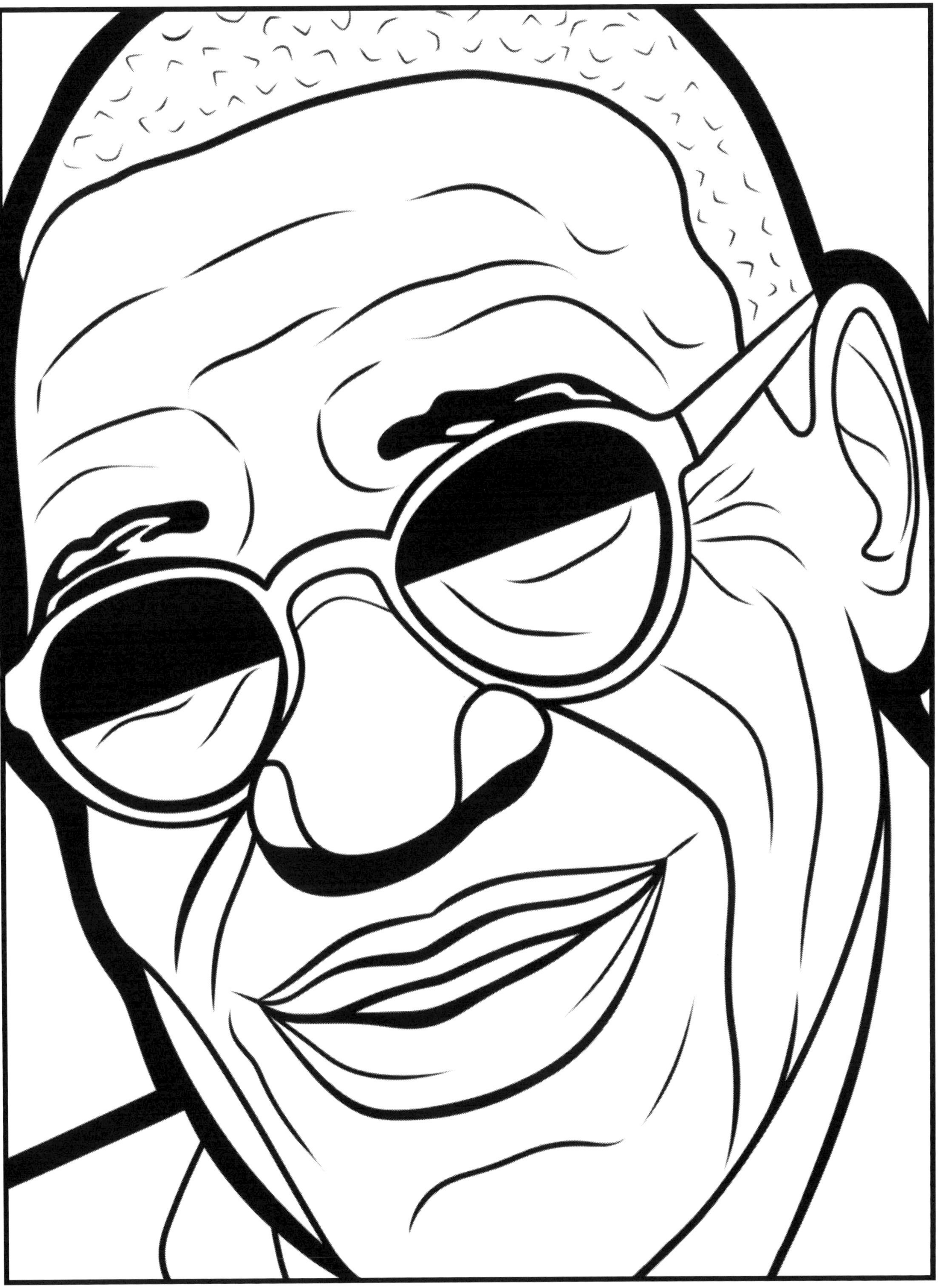

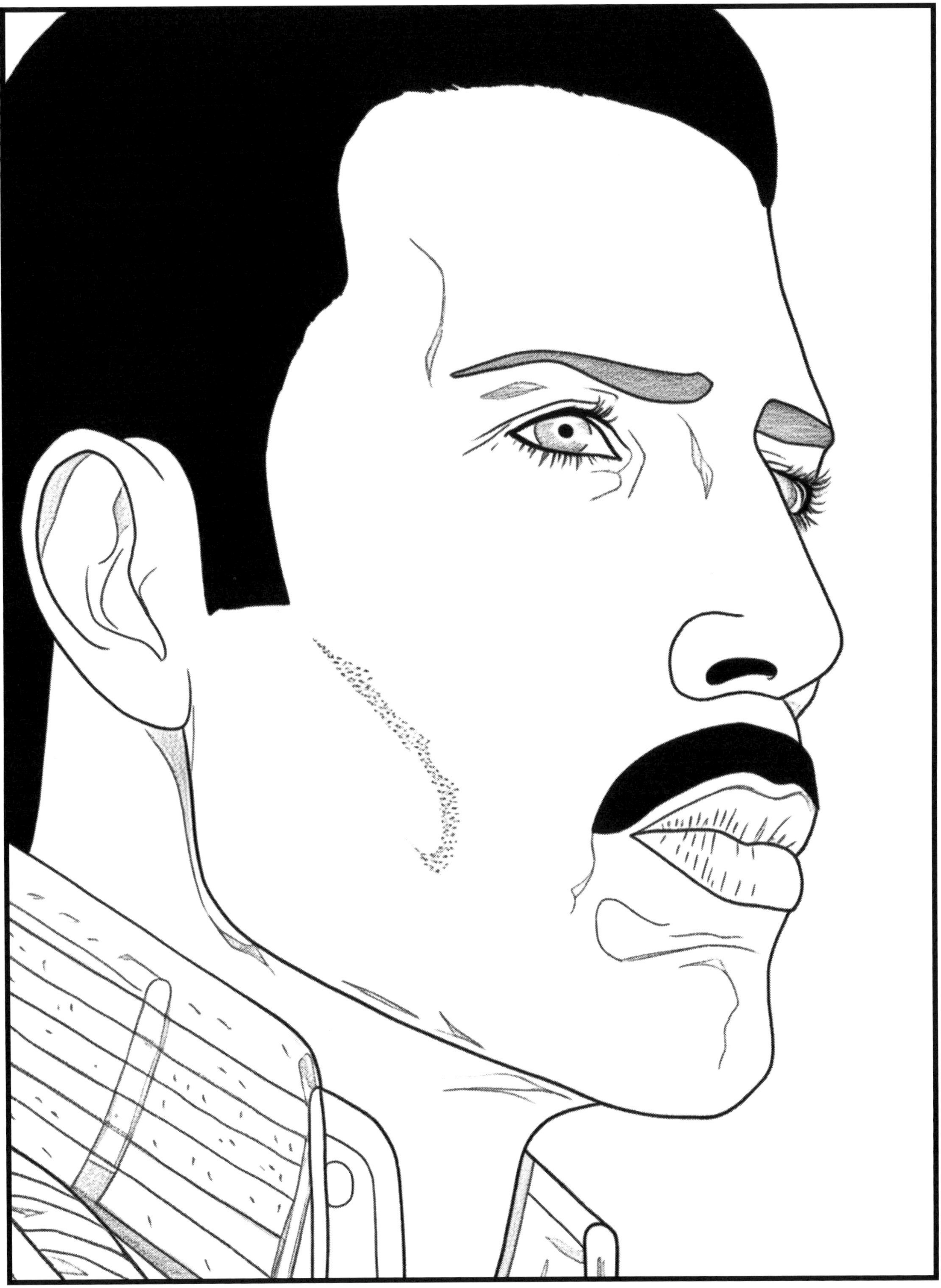

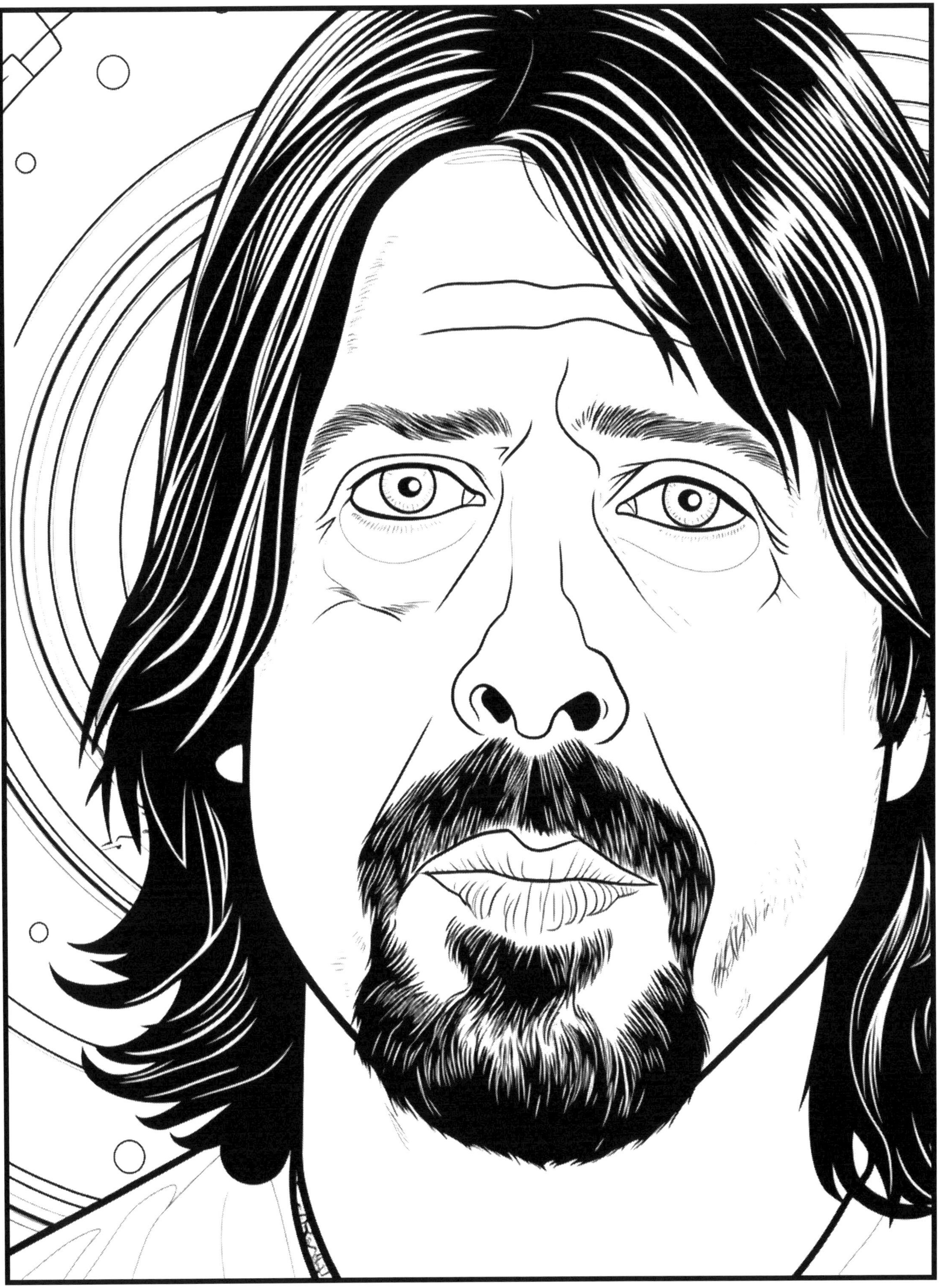

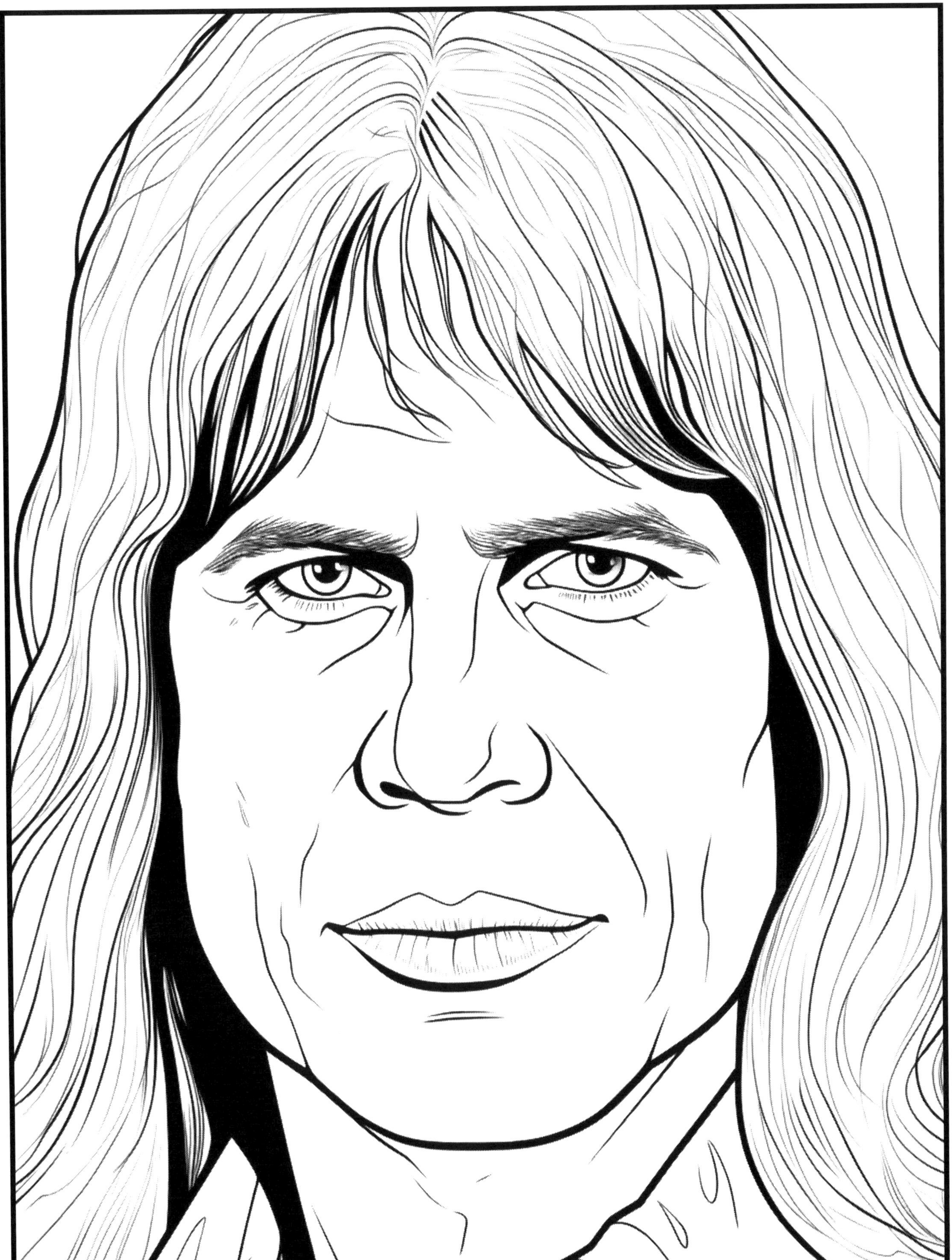

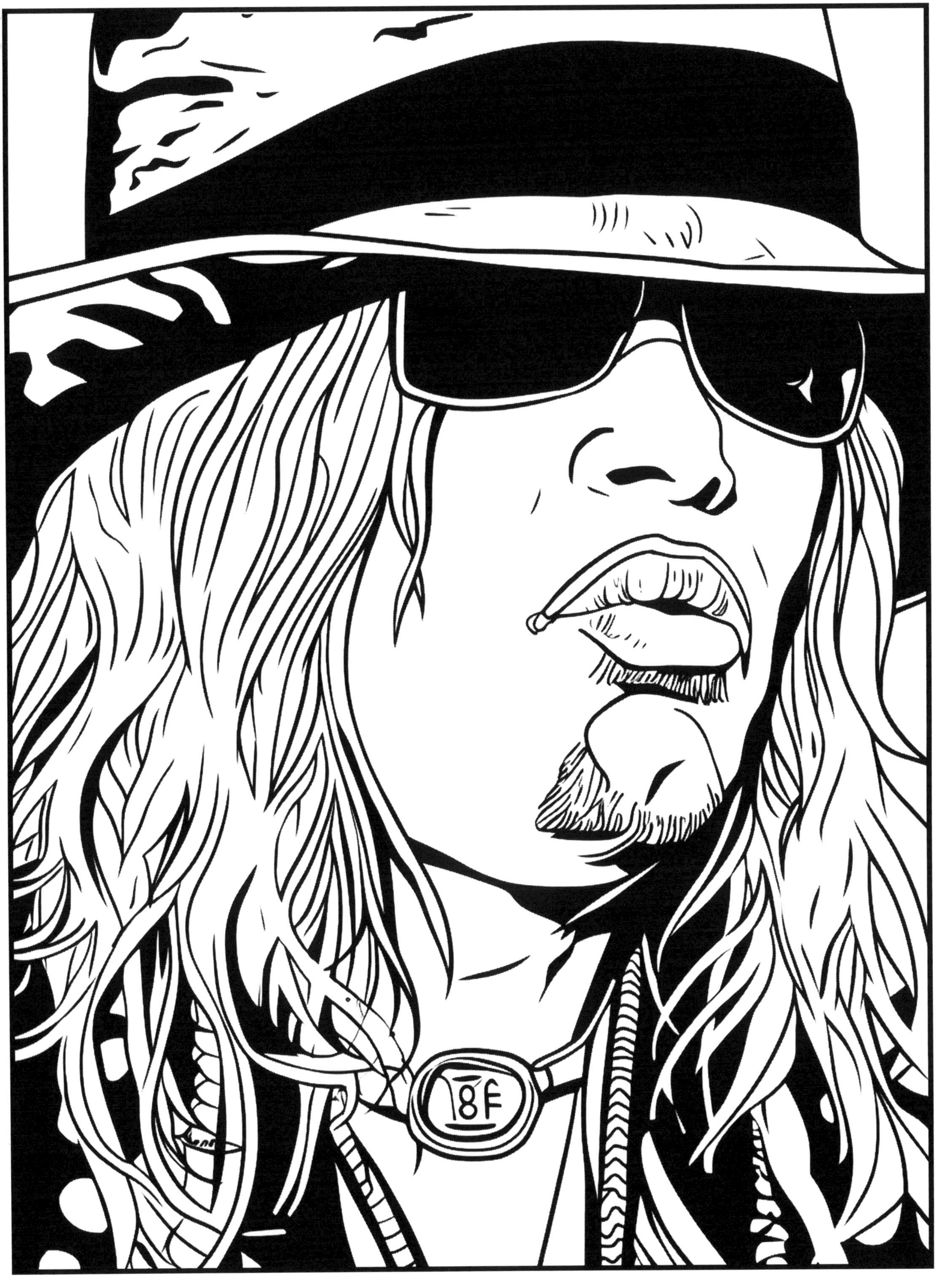
18F

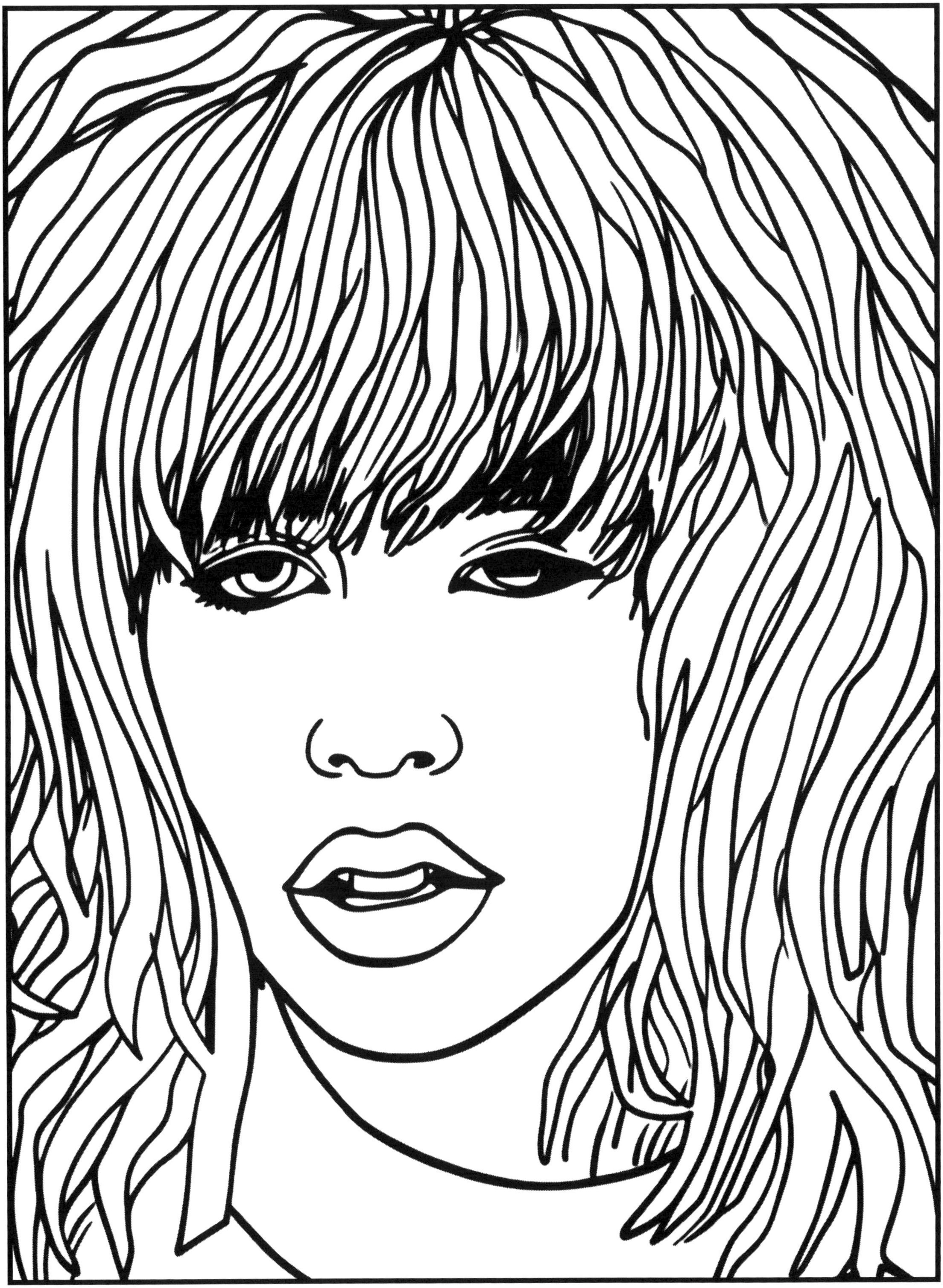

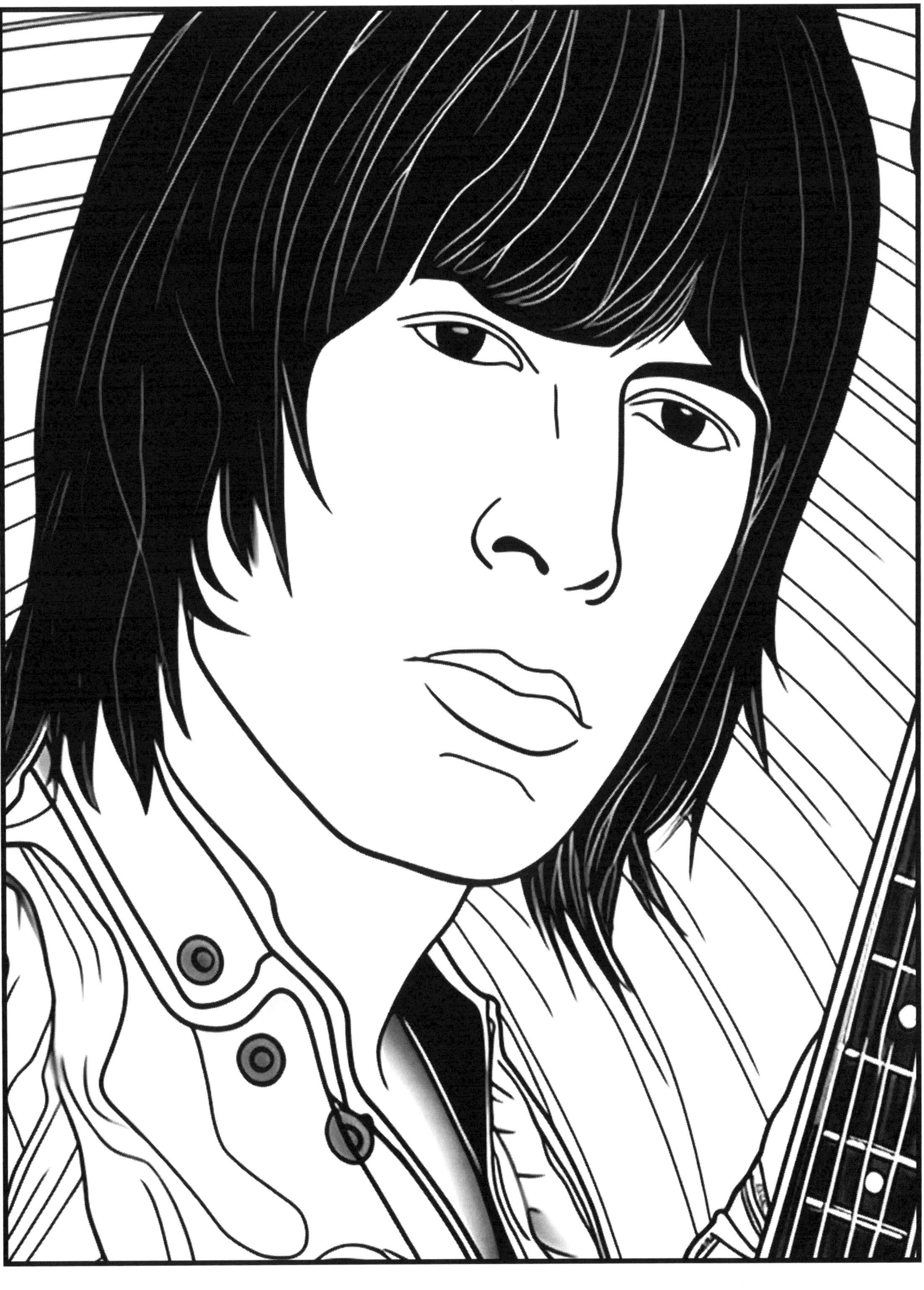

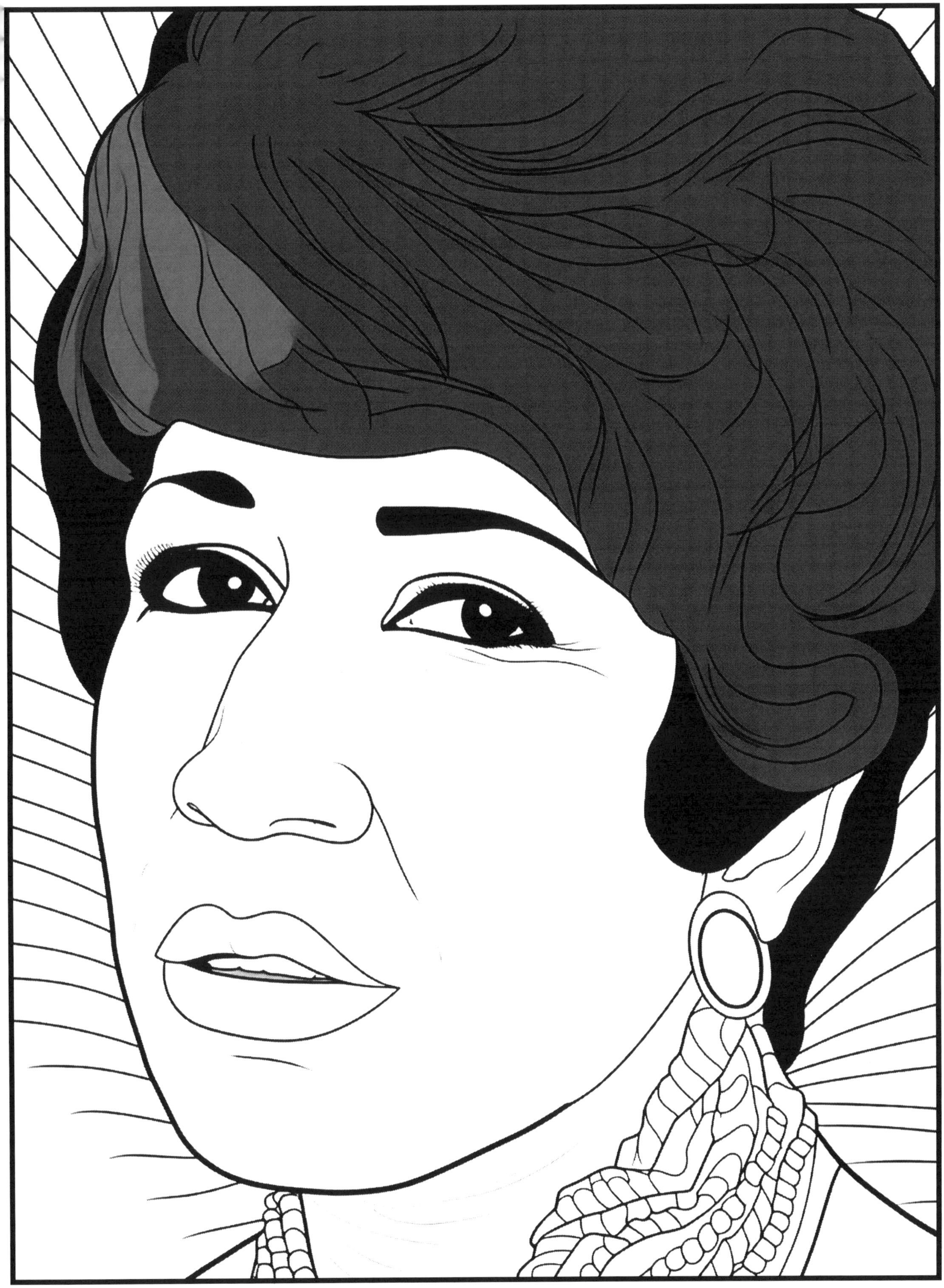

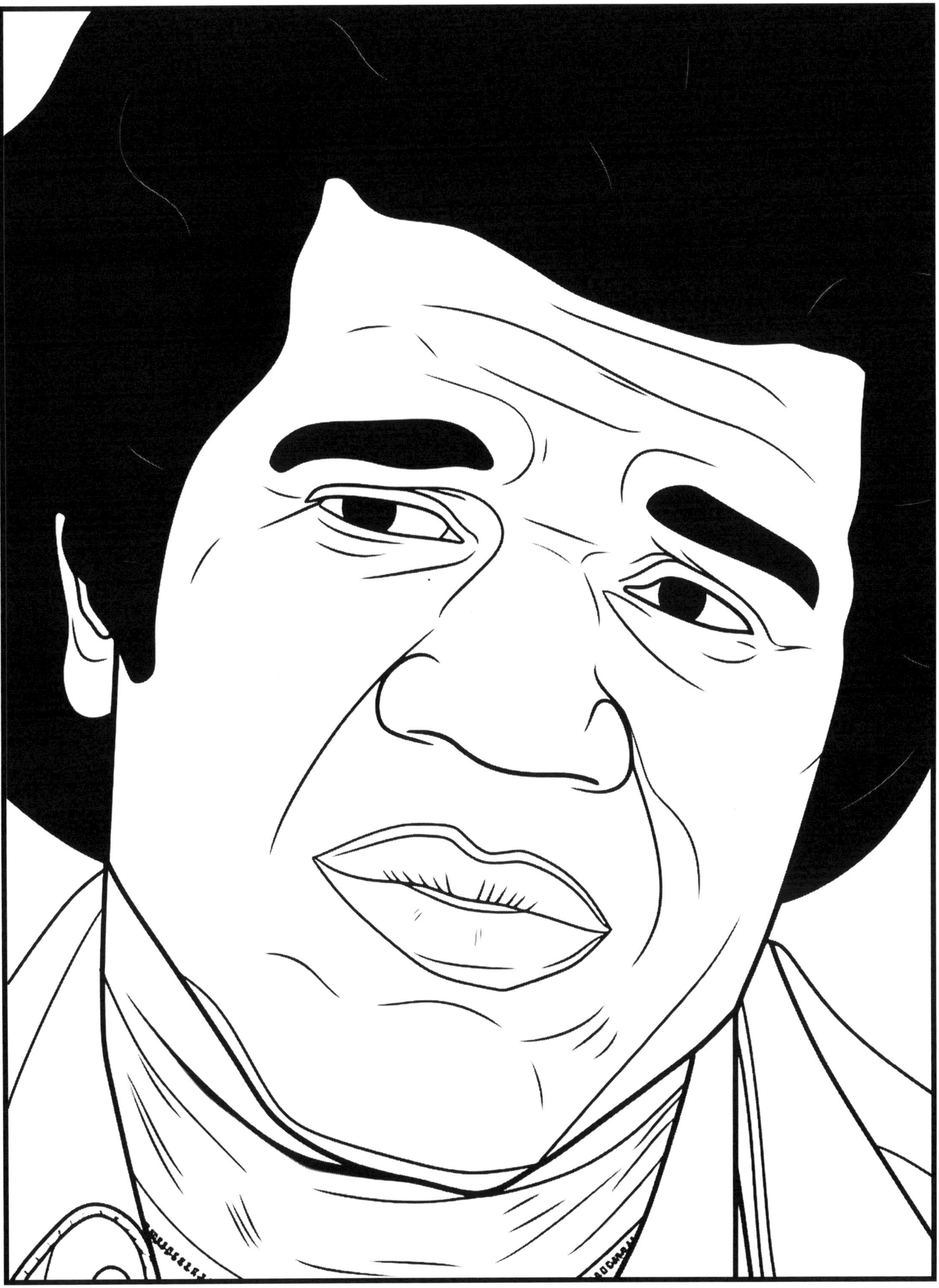

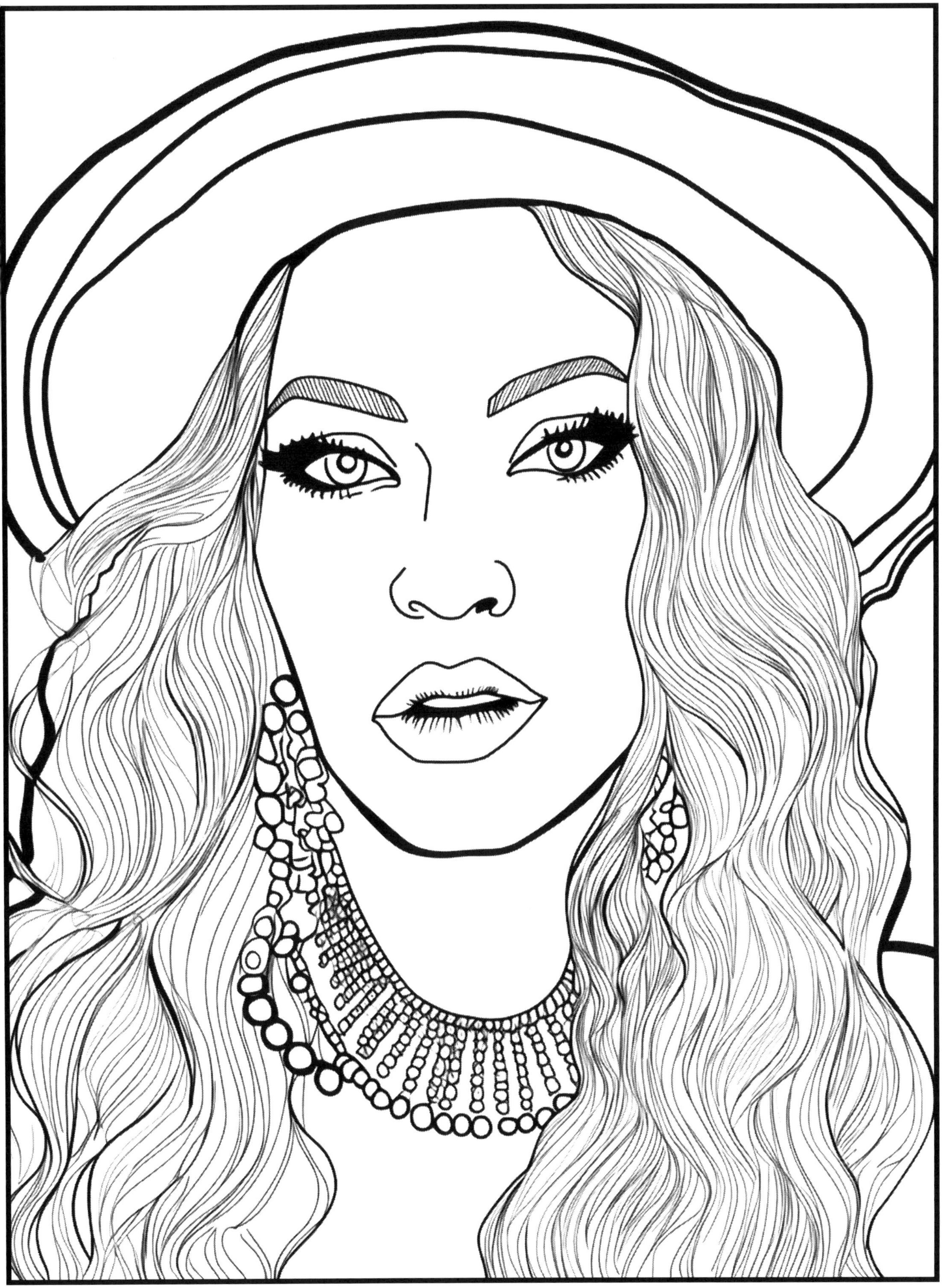

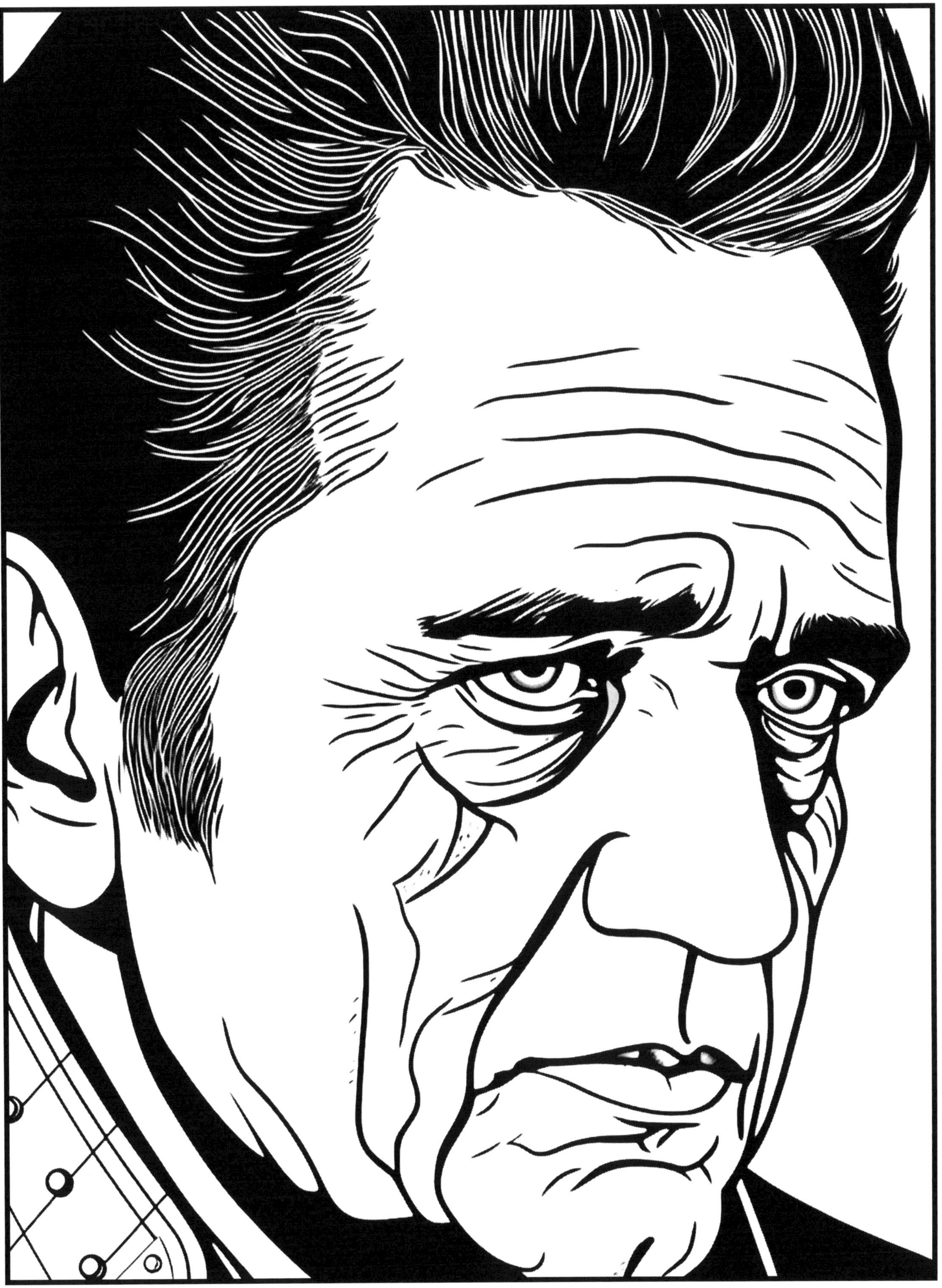

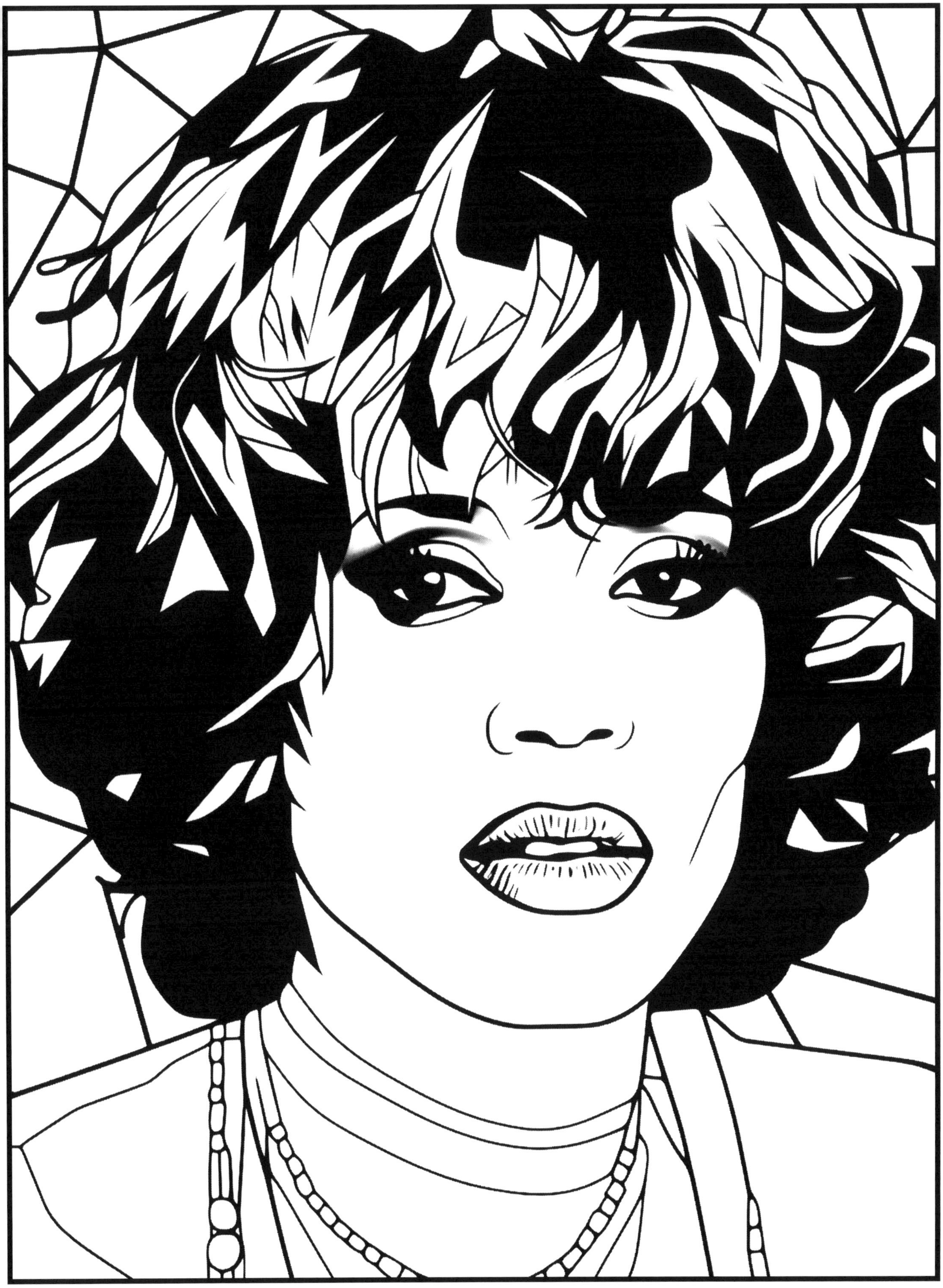

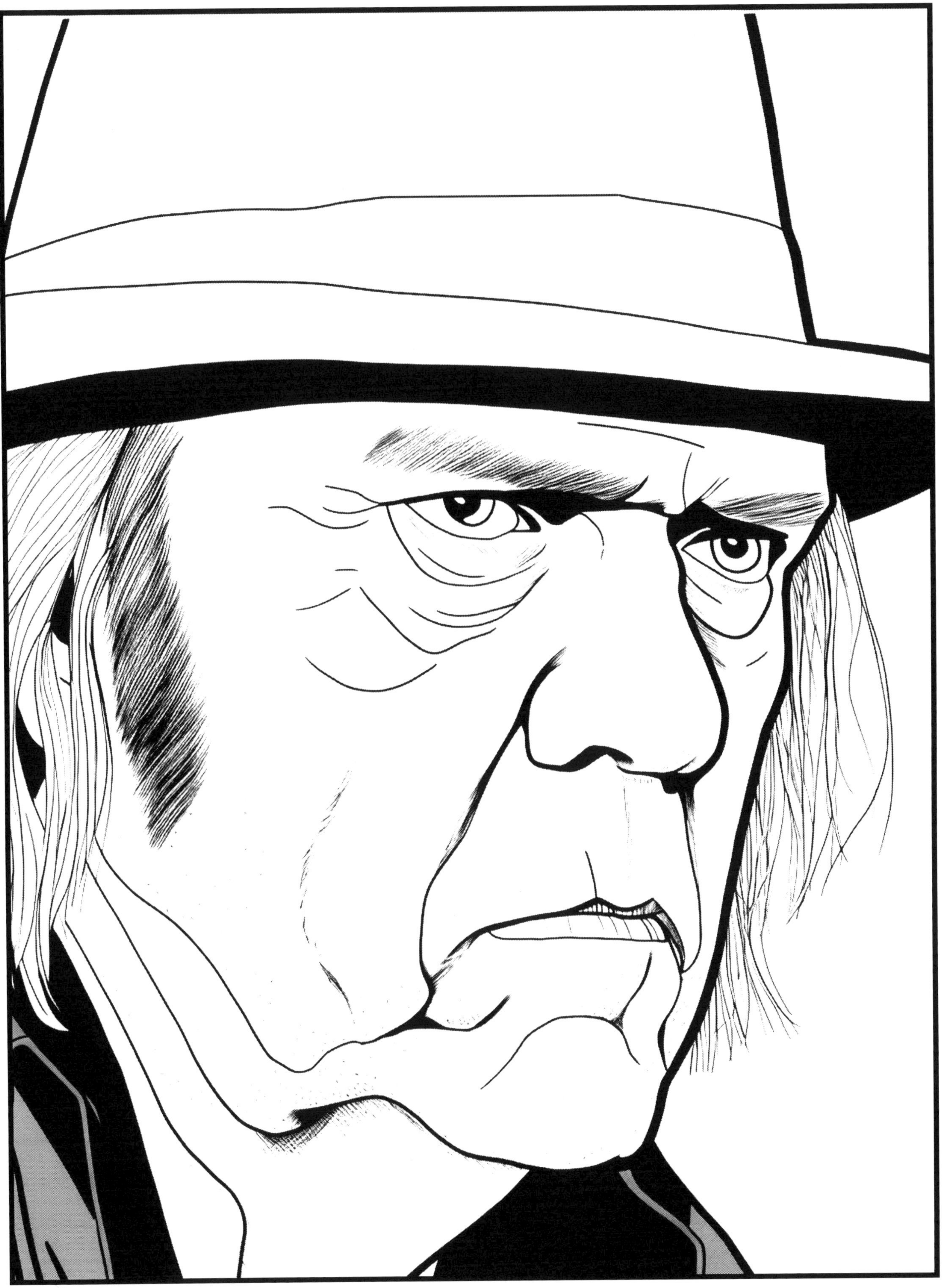

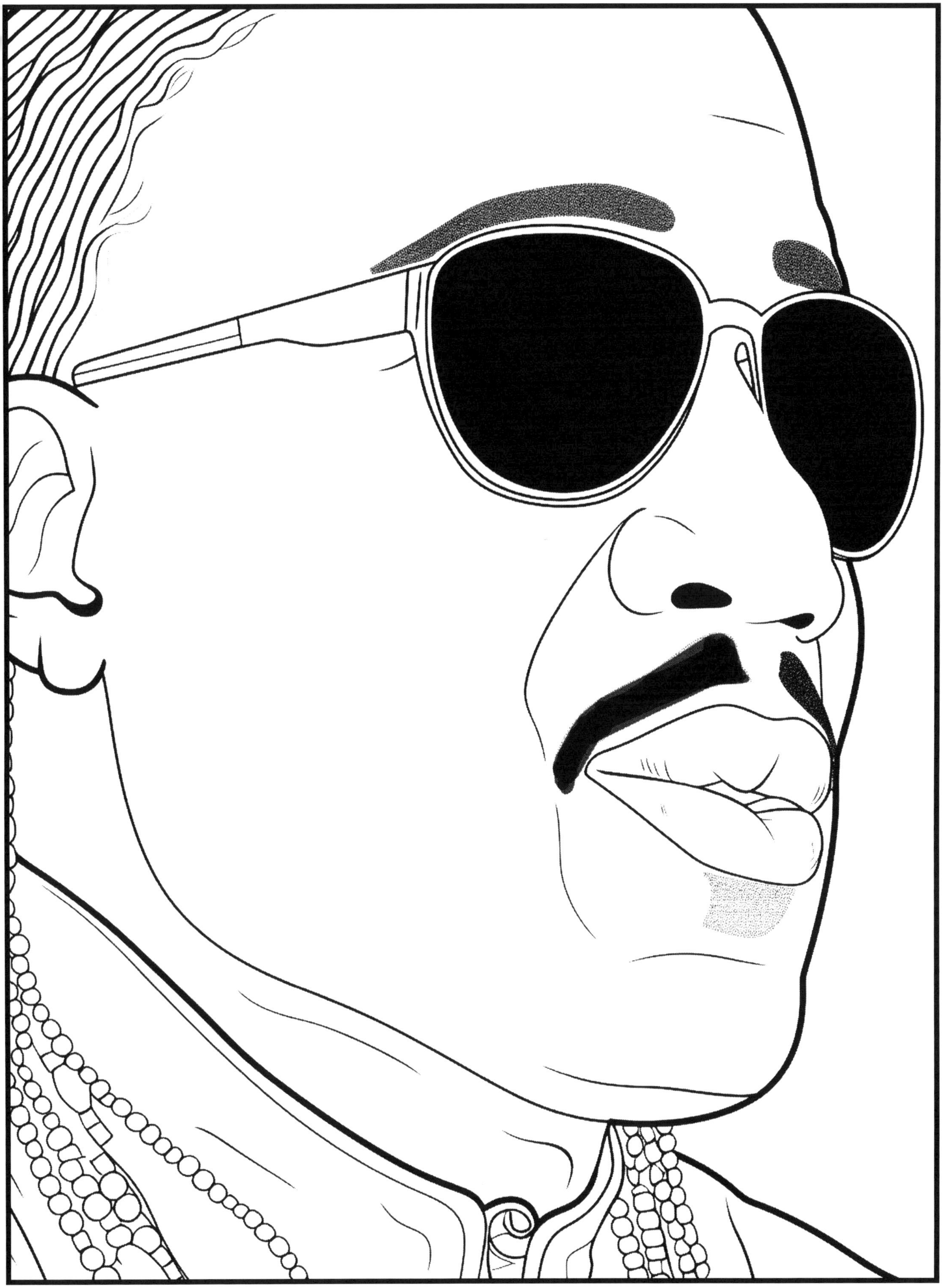

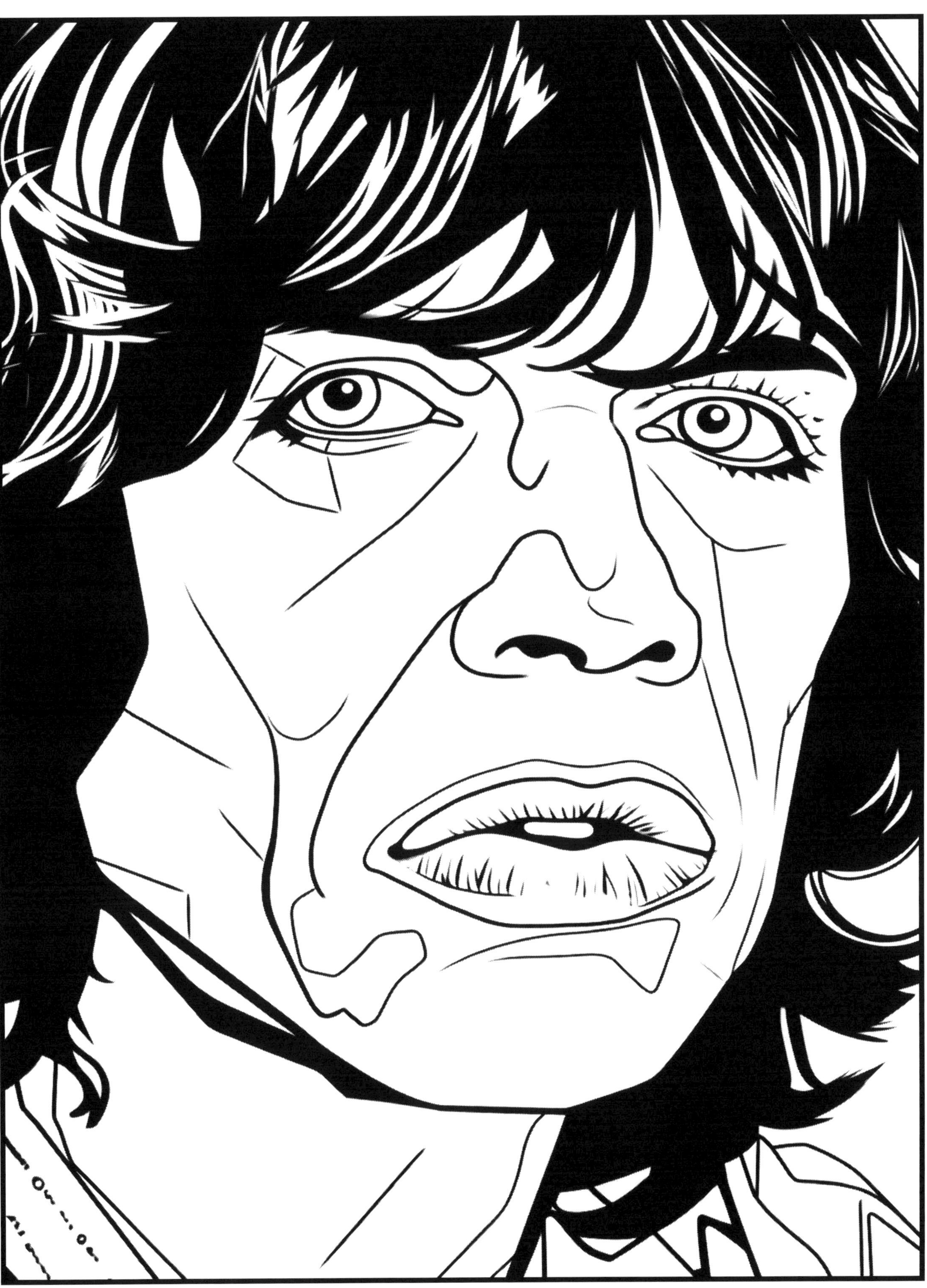

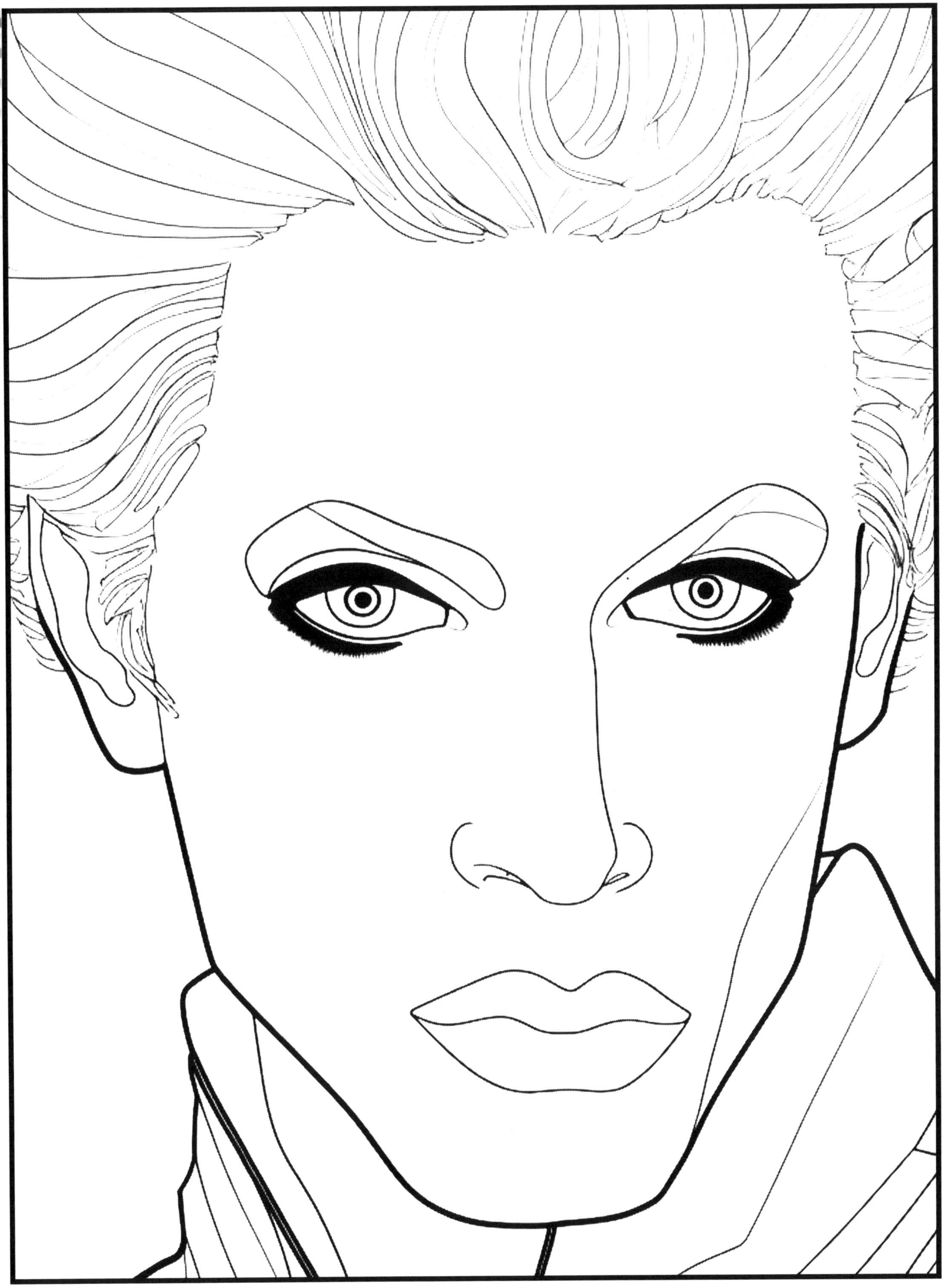

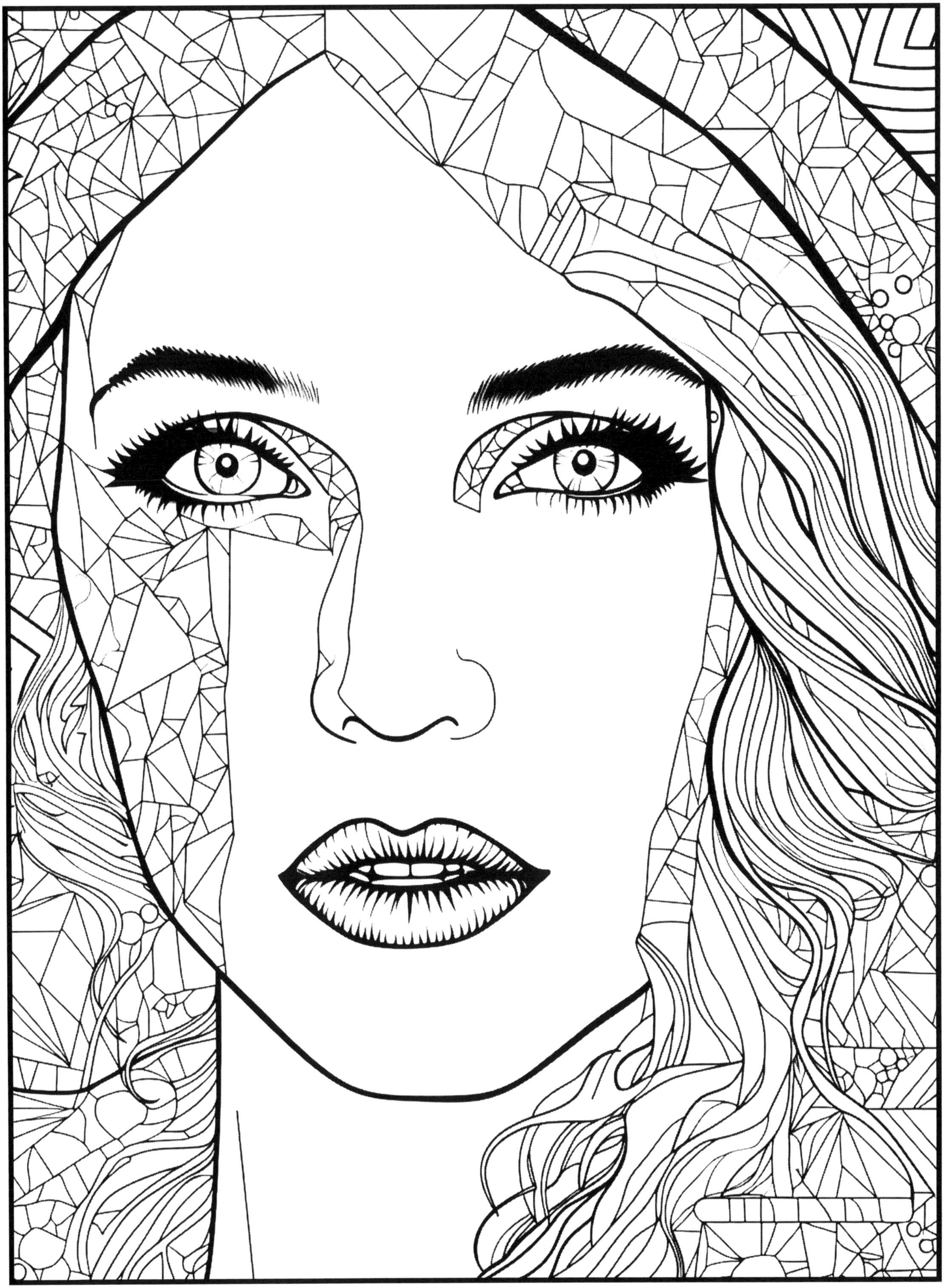

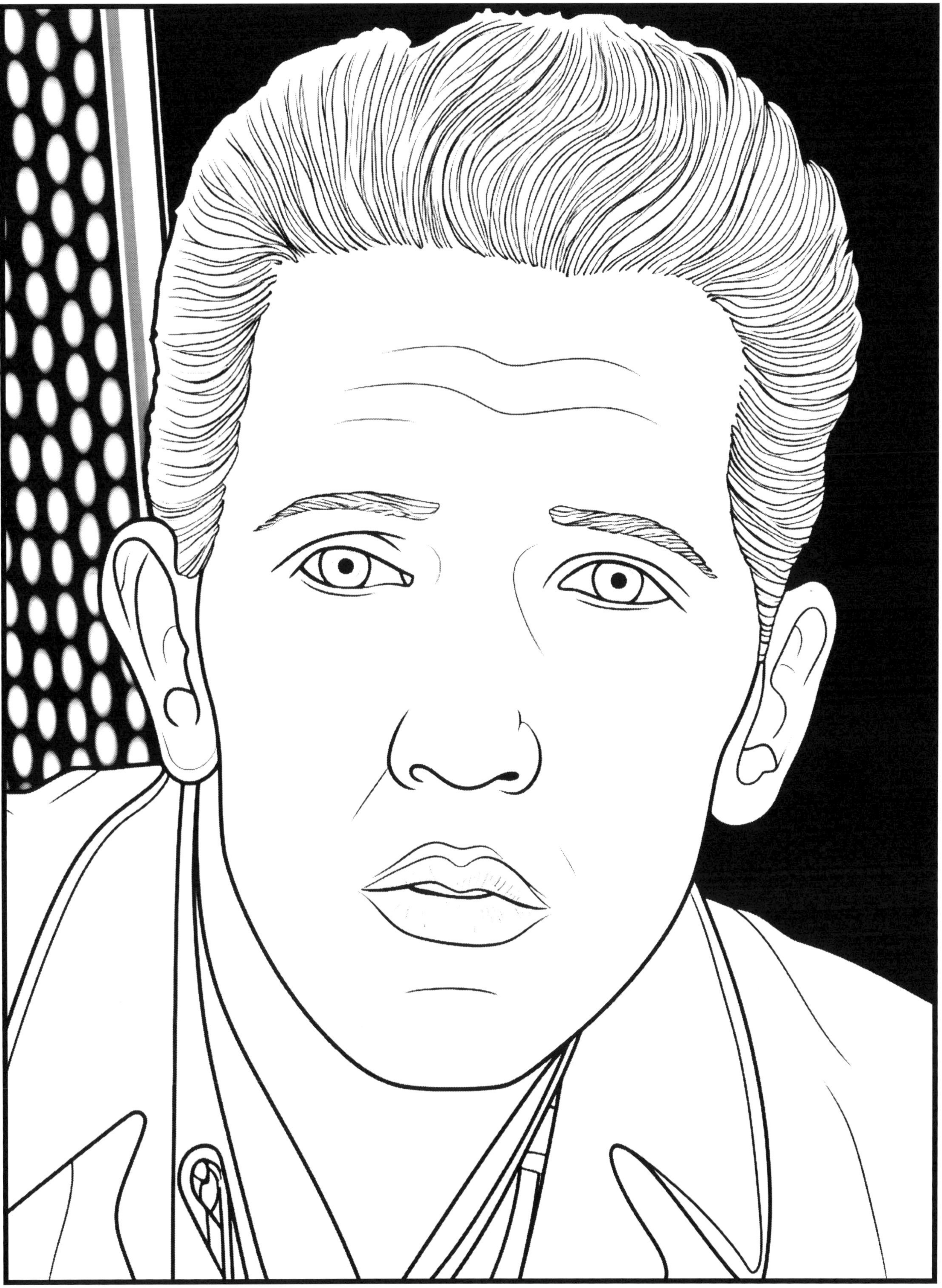

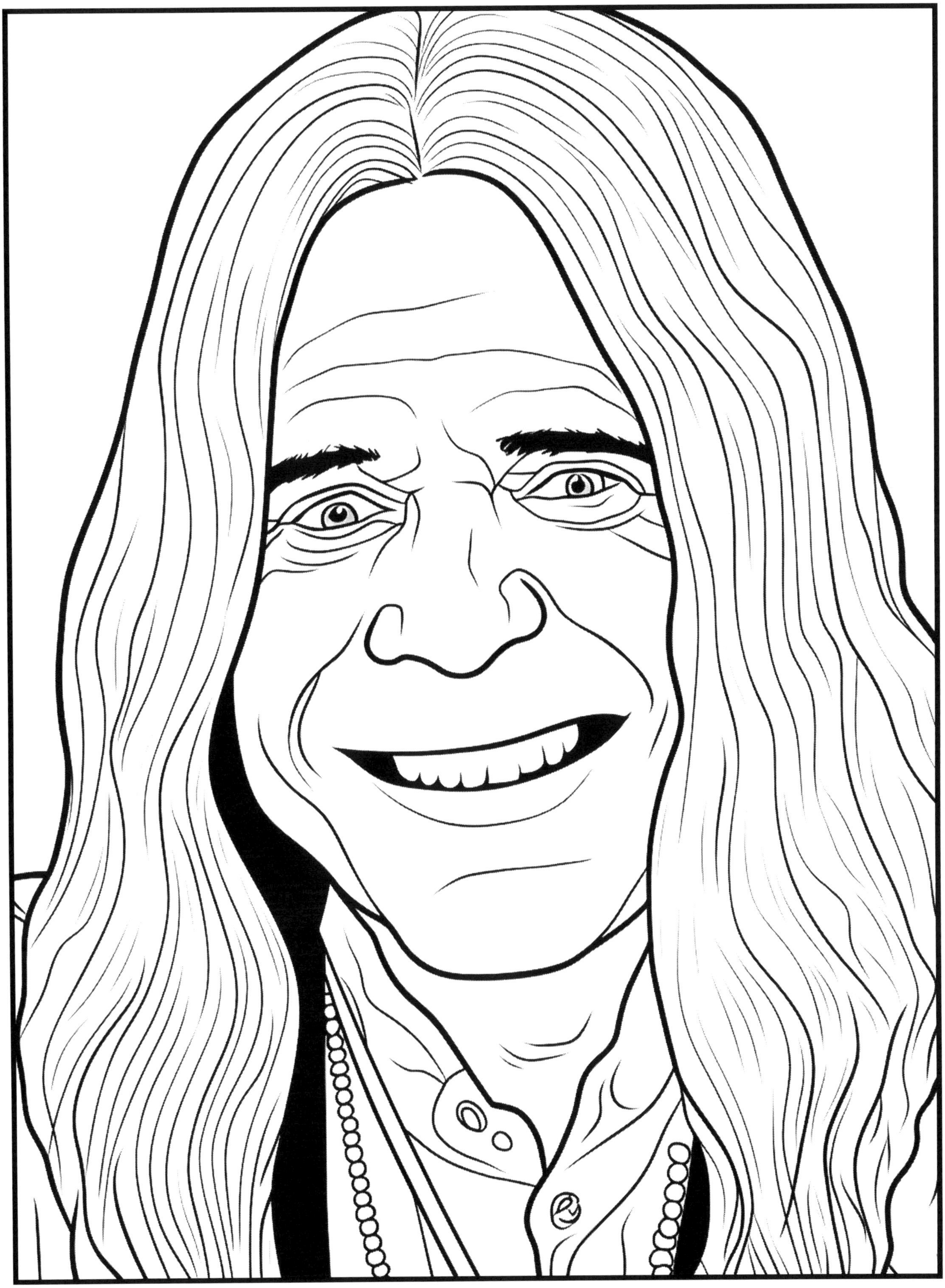

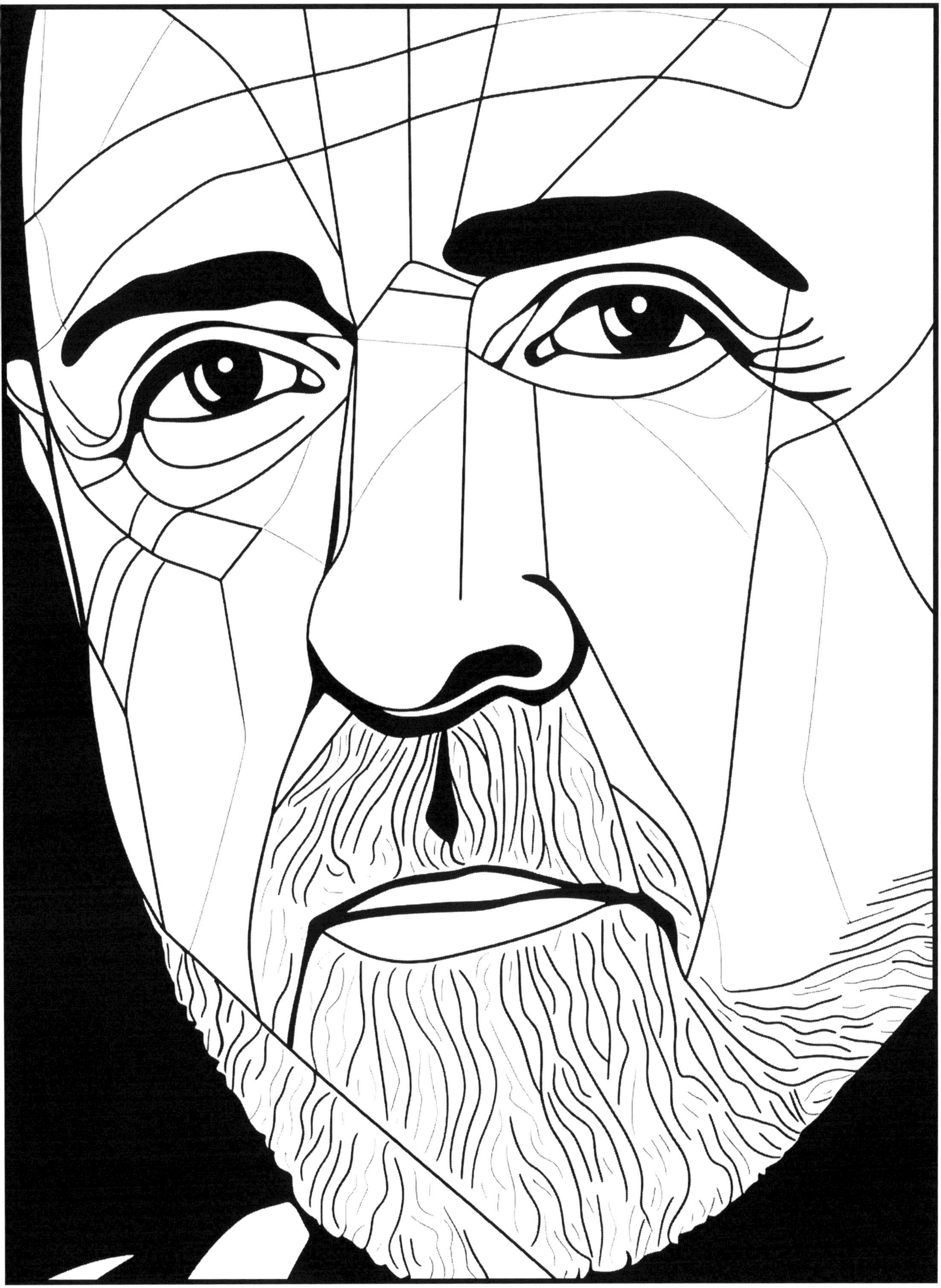

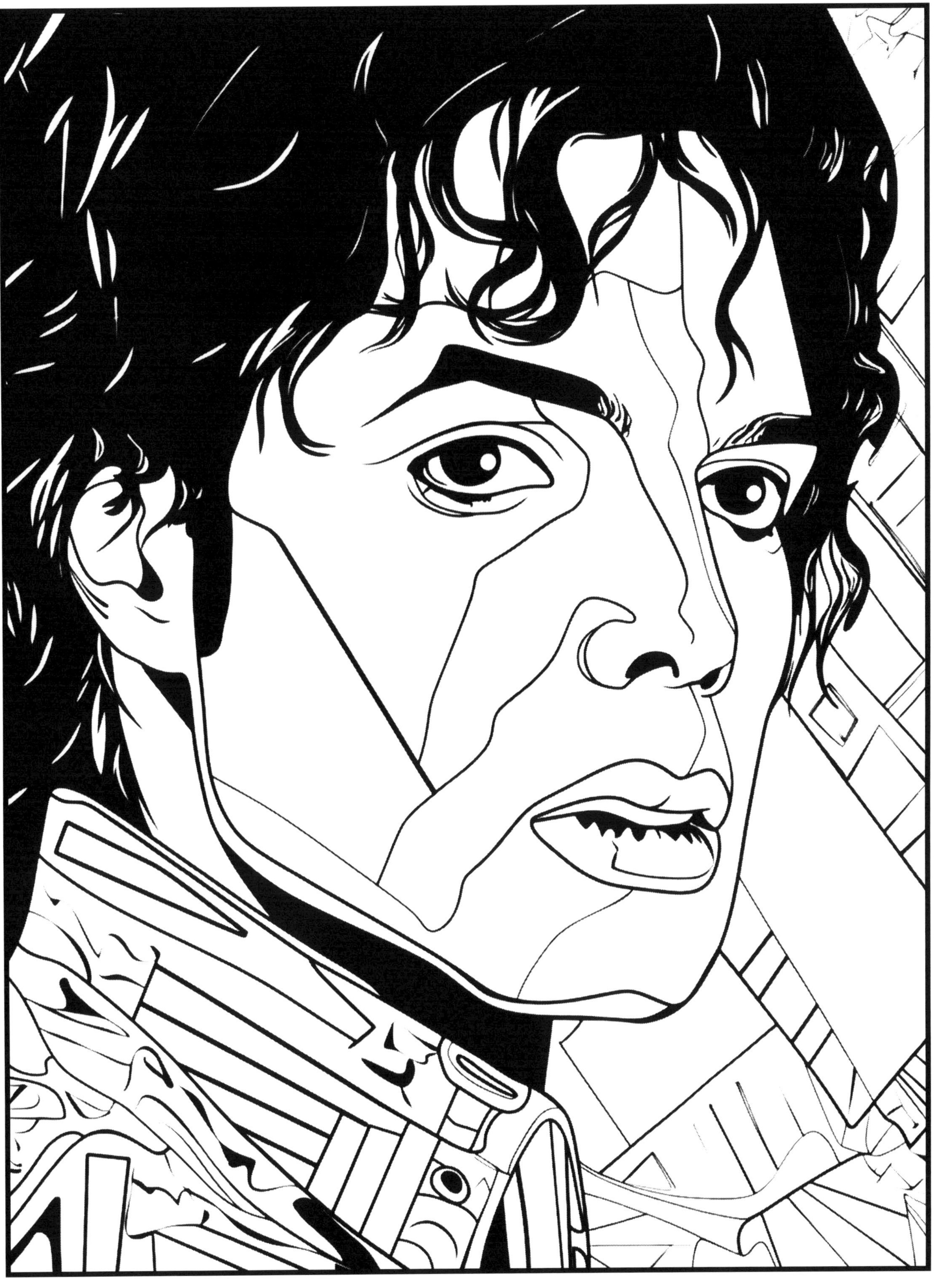

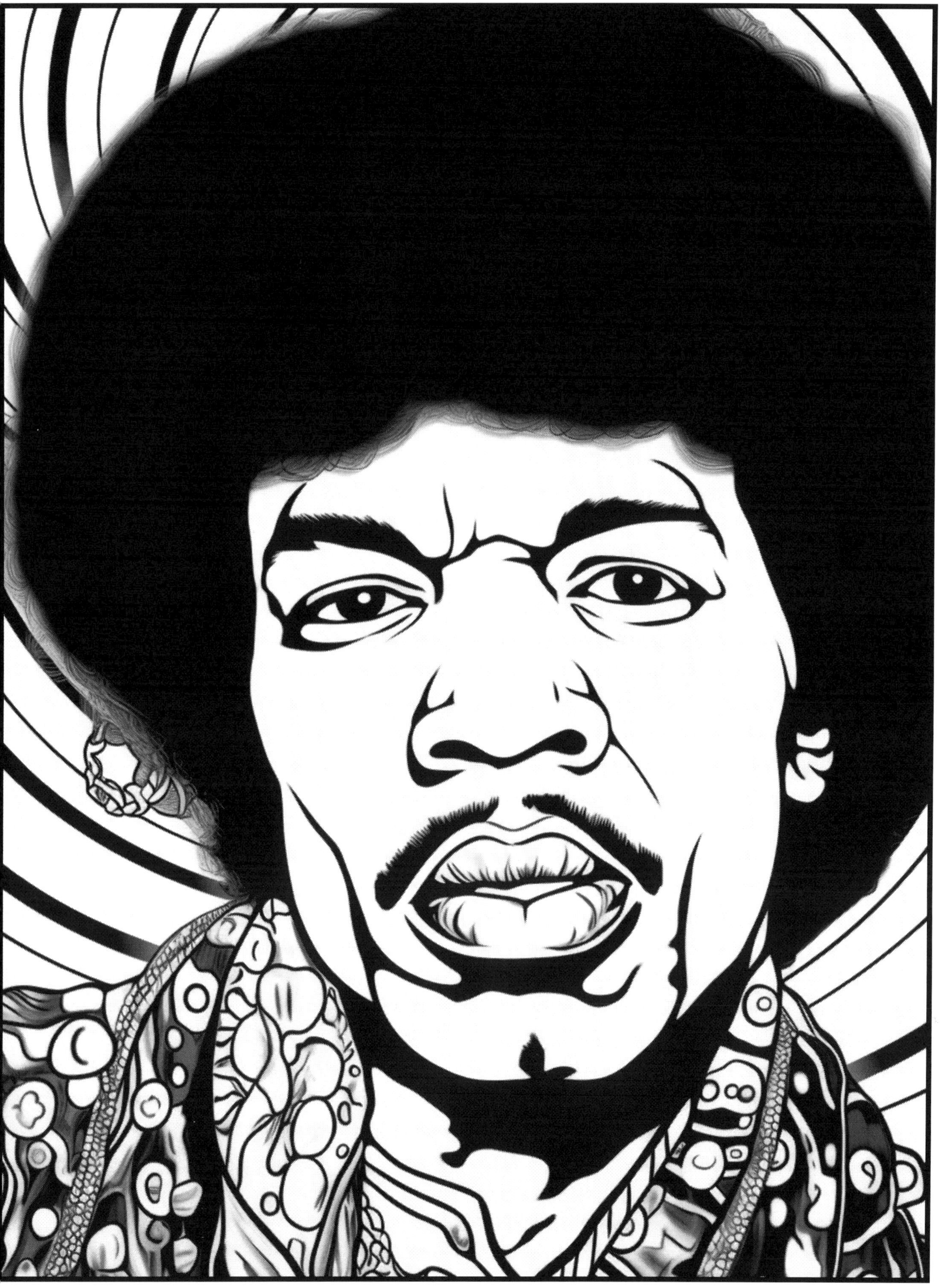

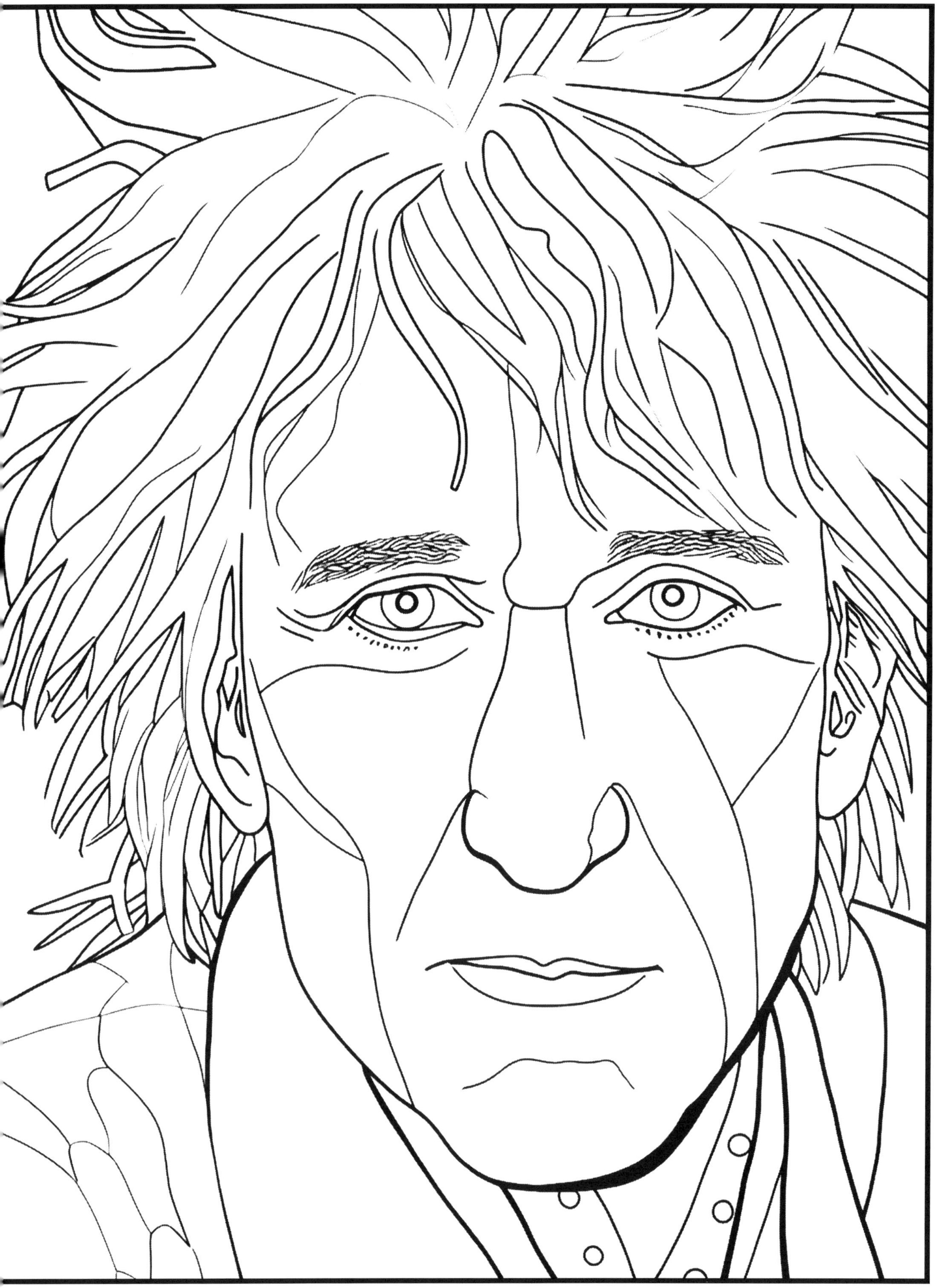

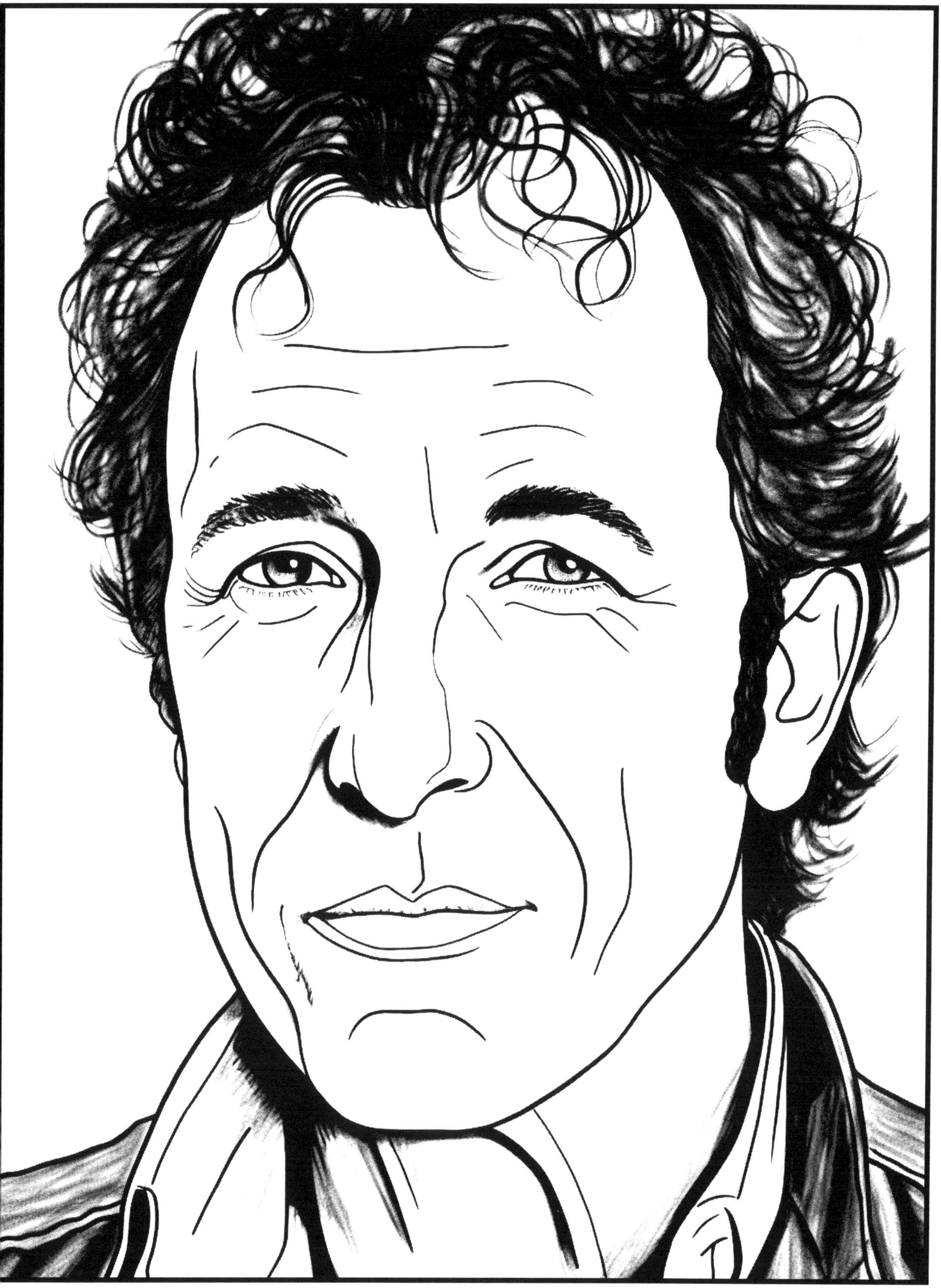

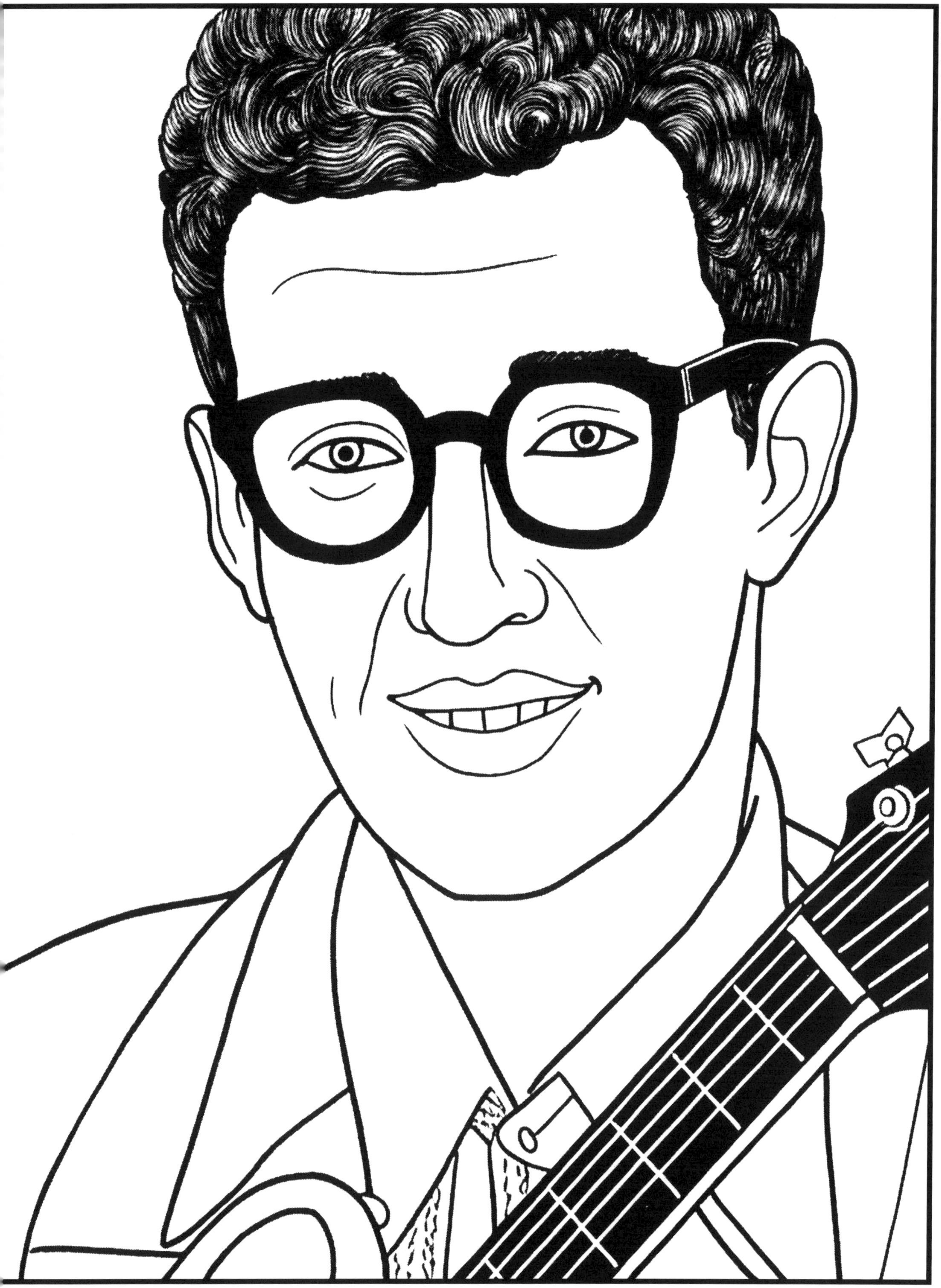

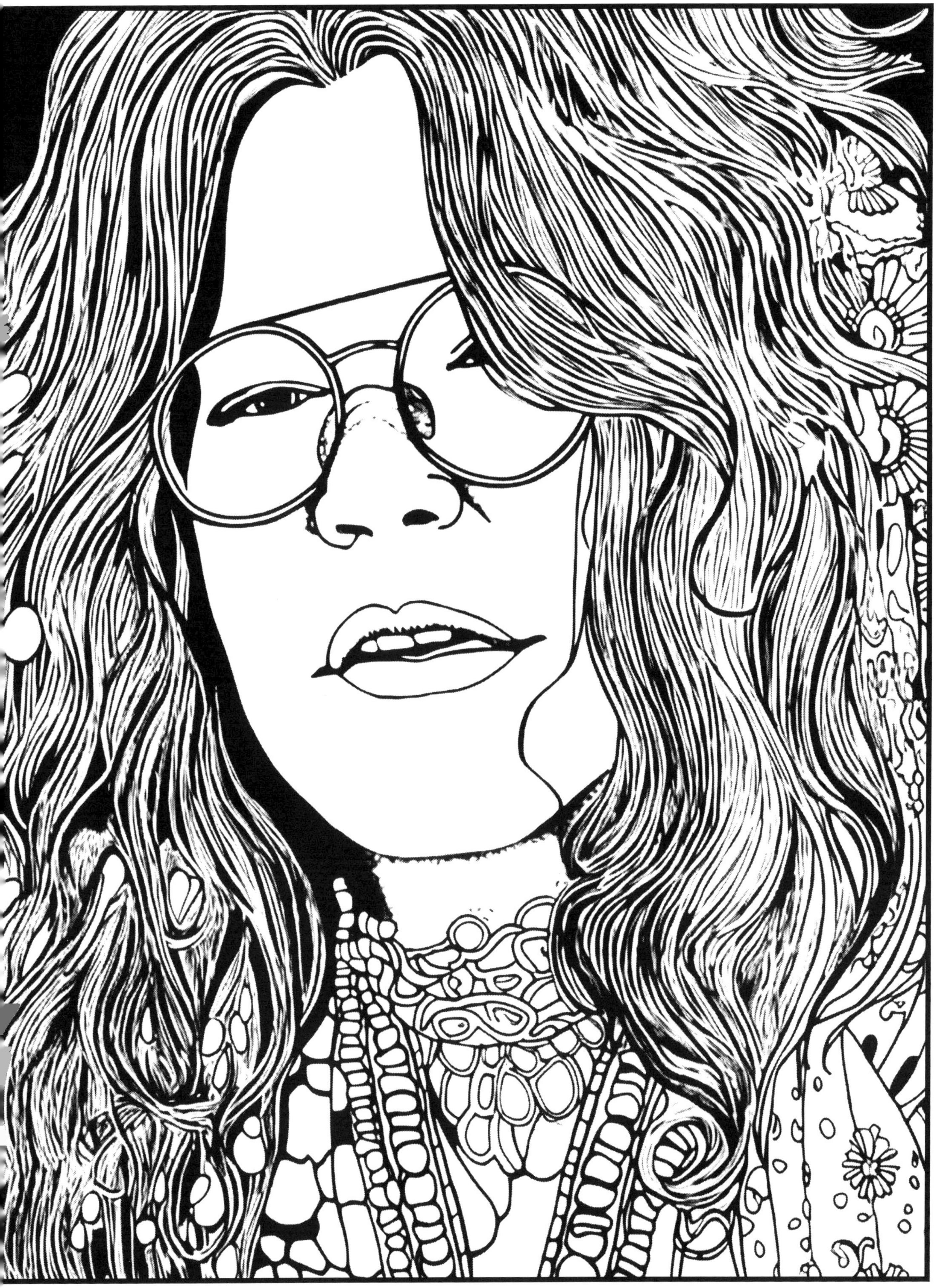

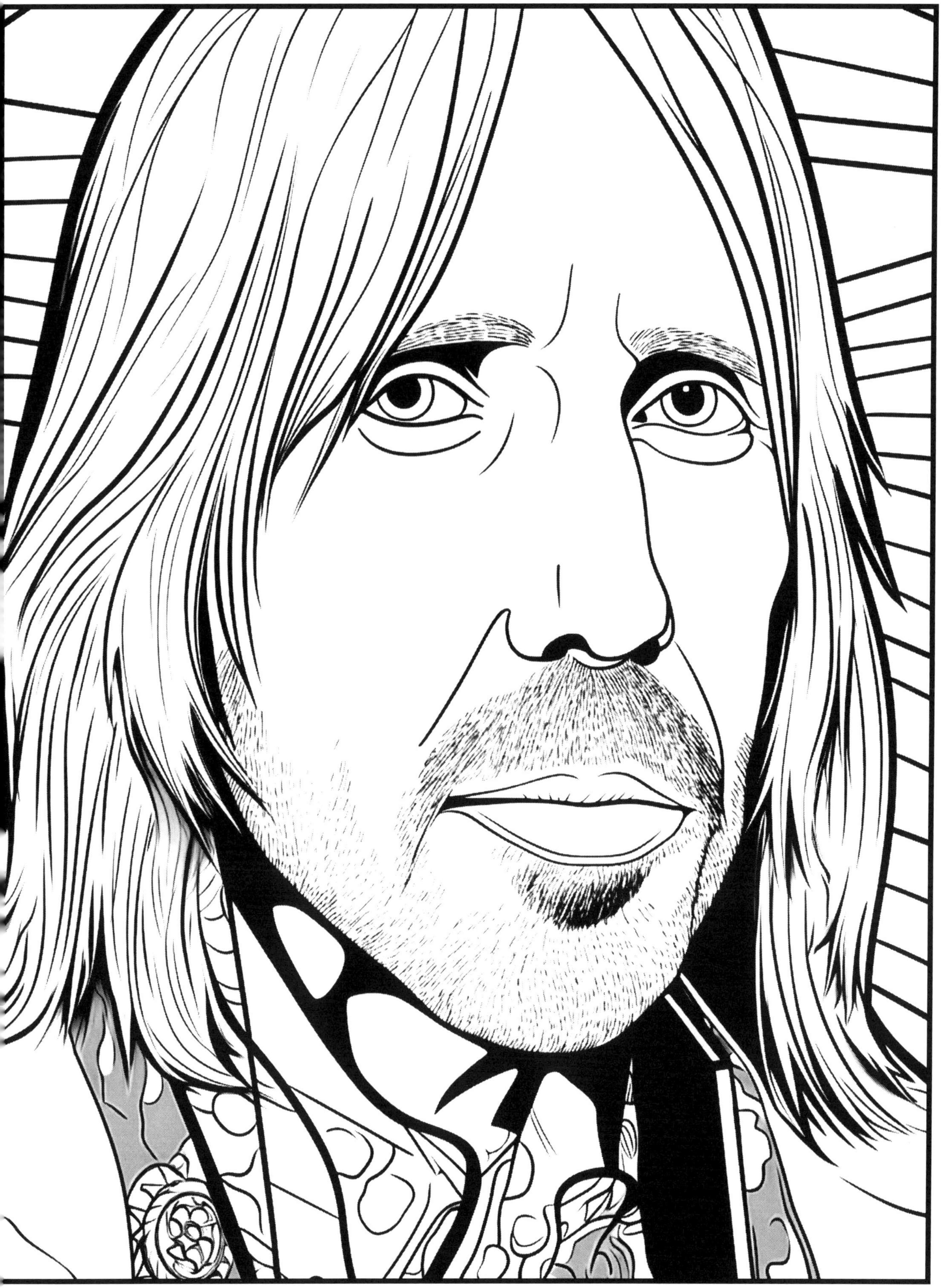

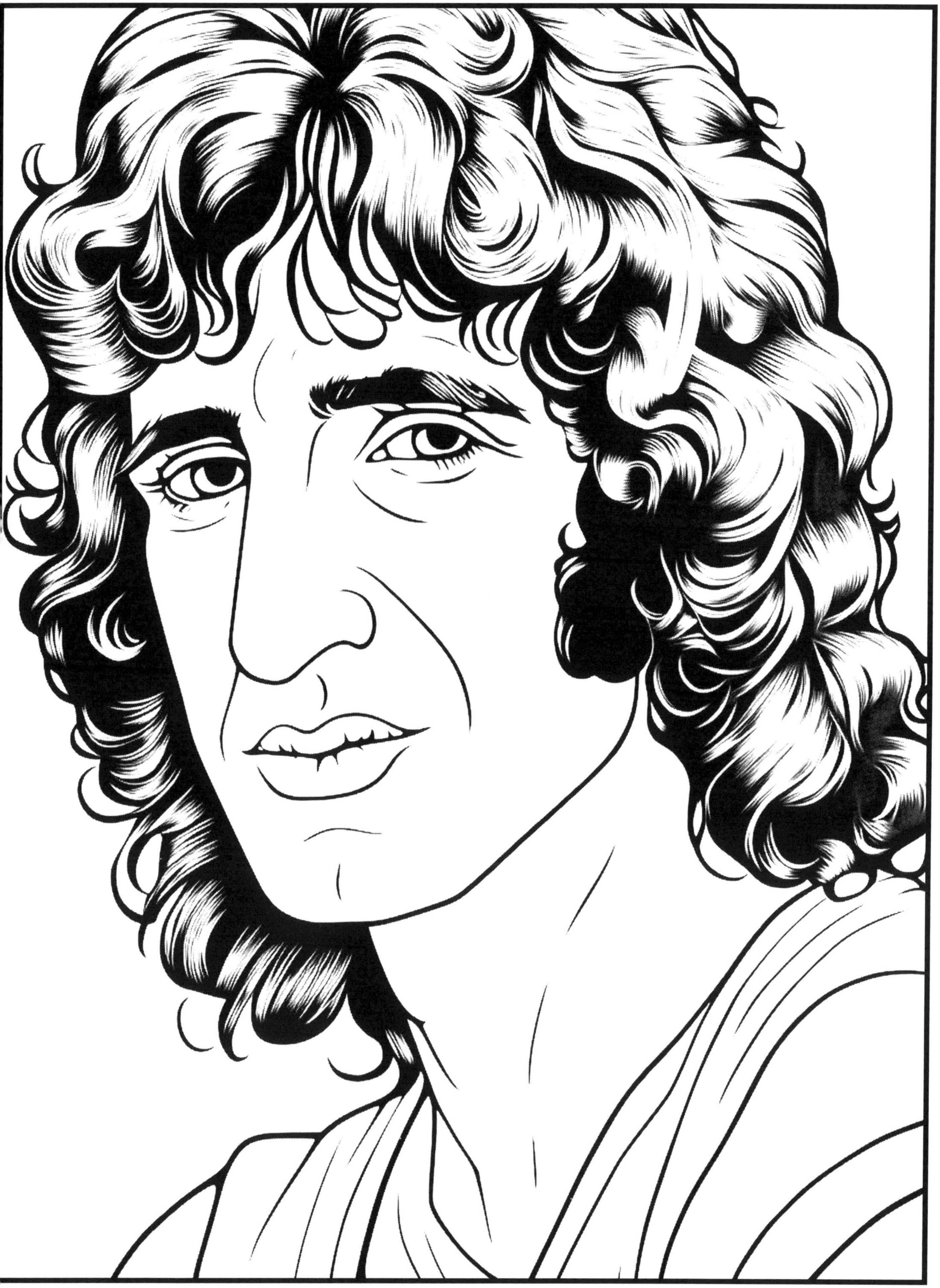

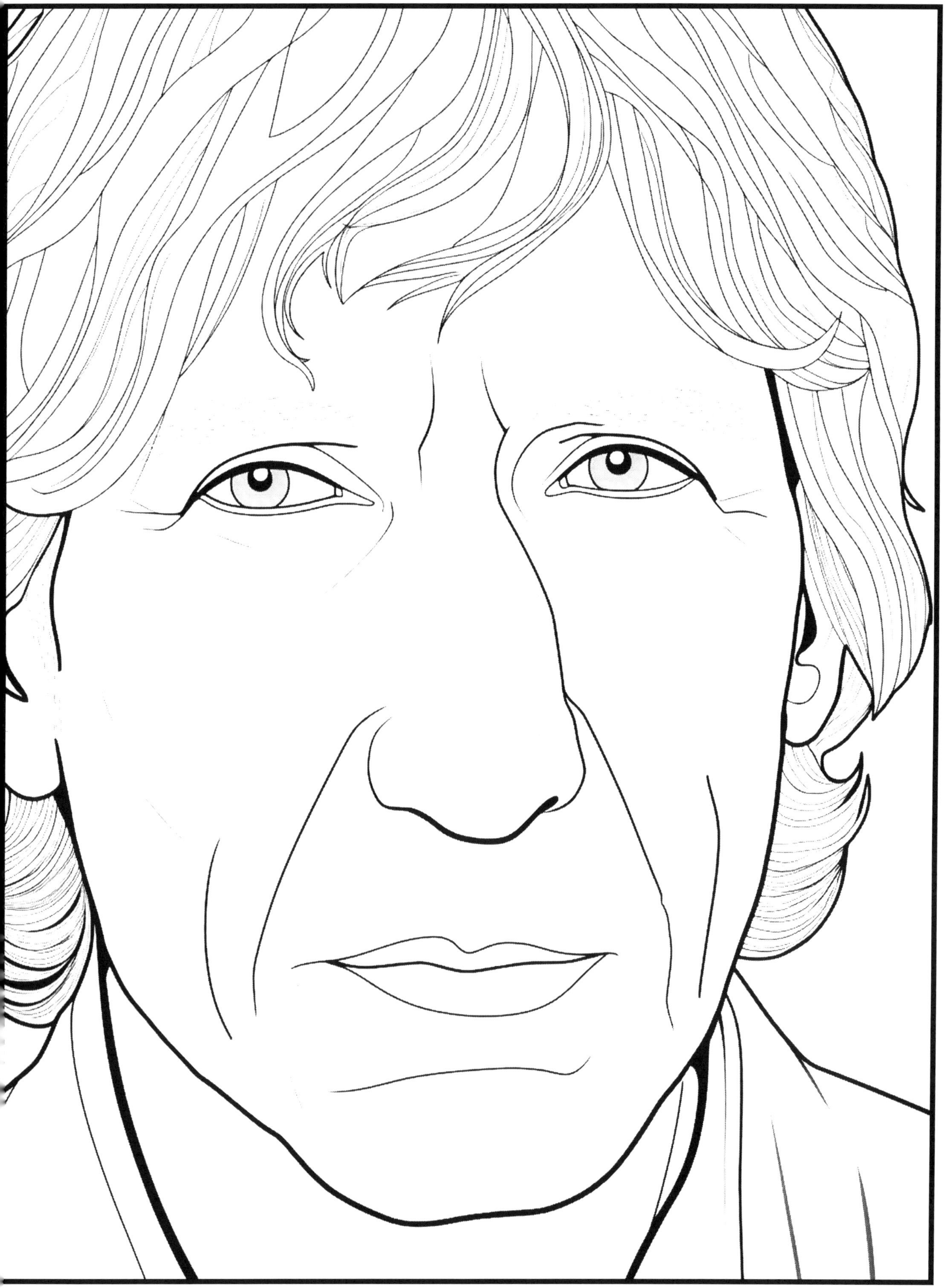

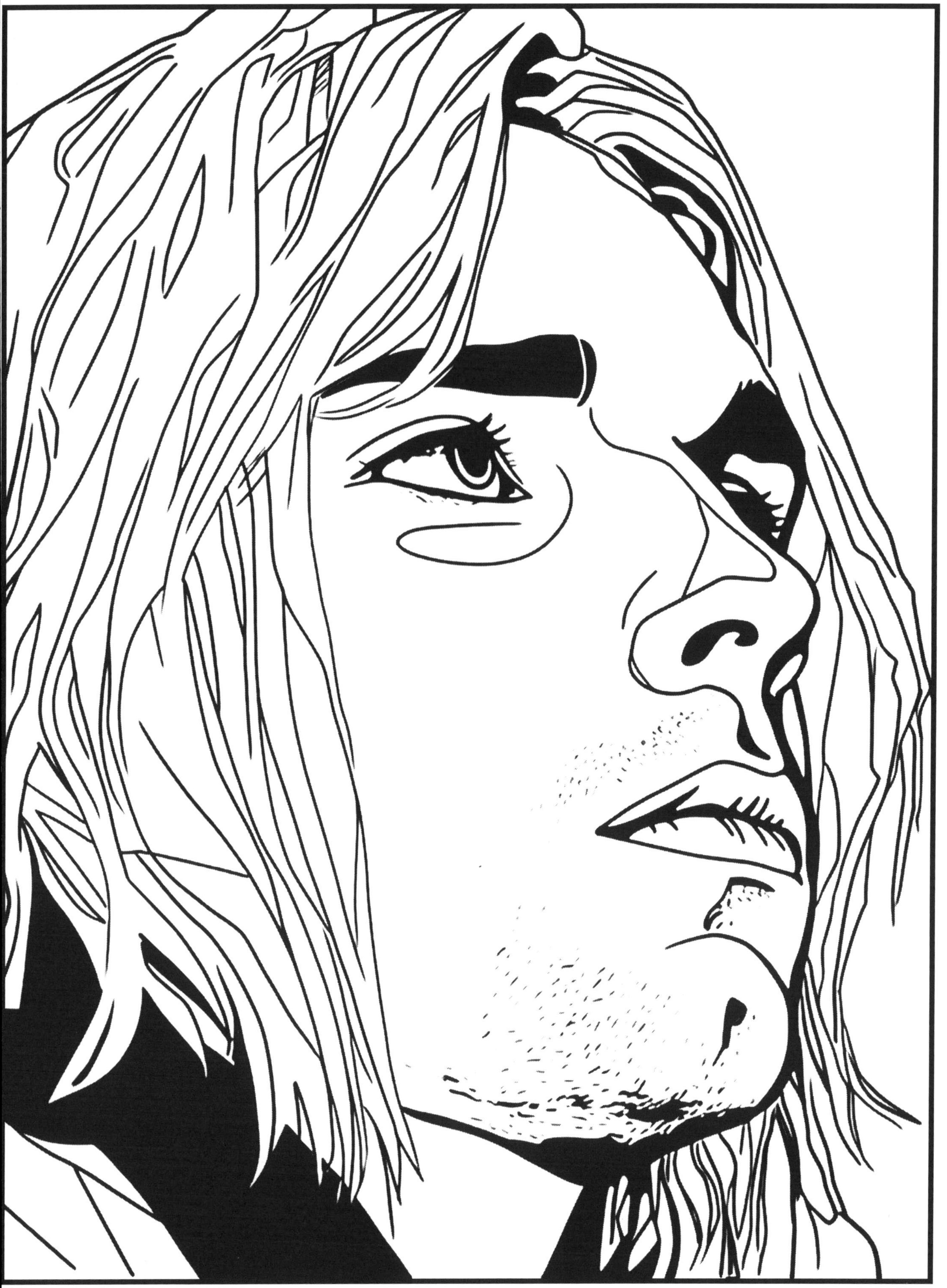

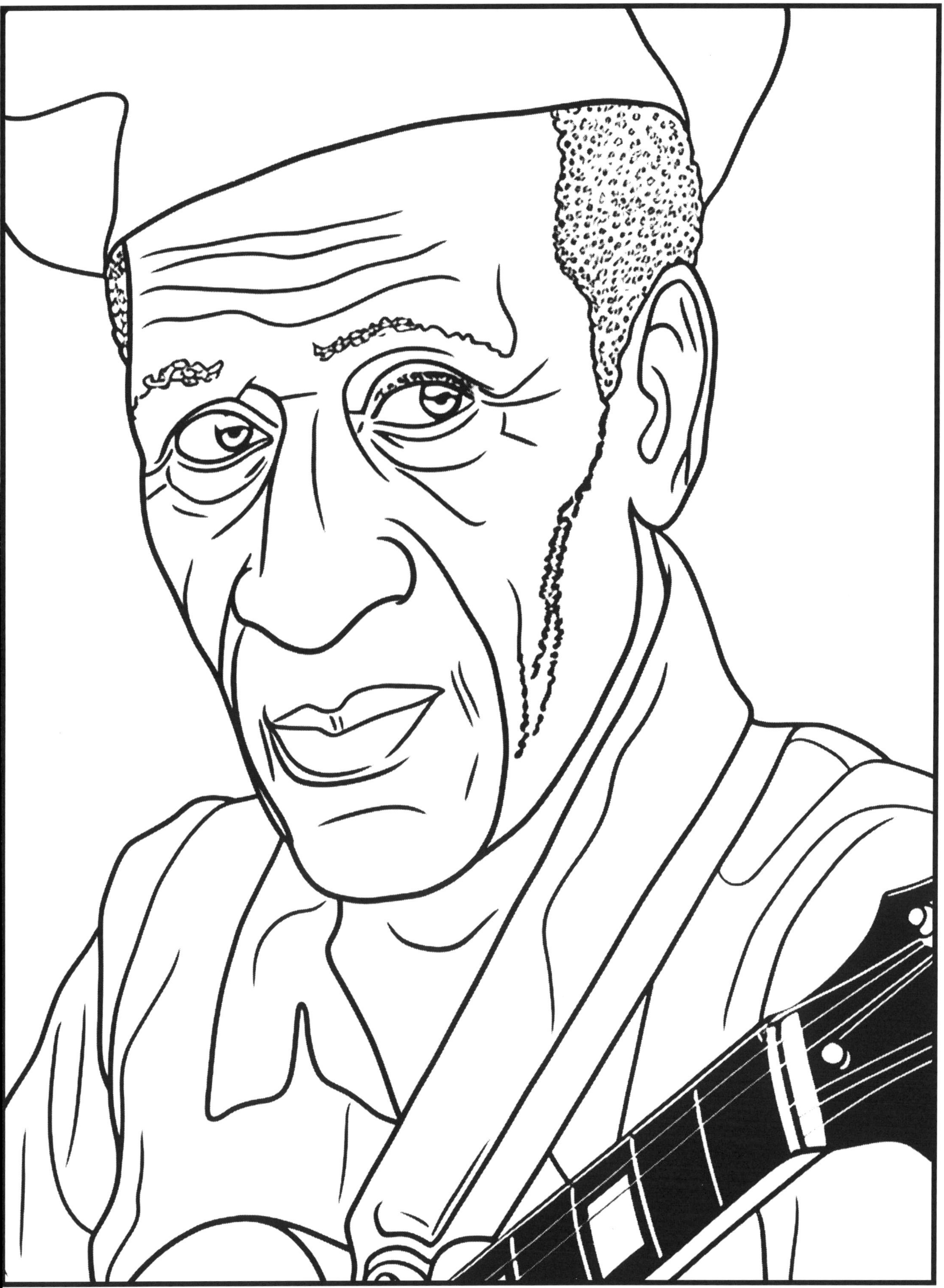

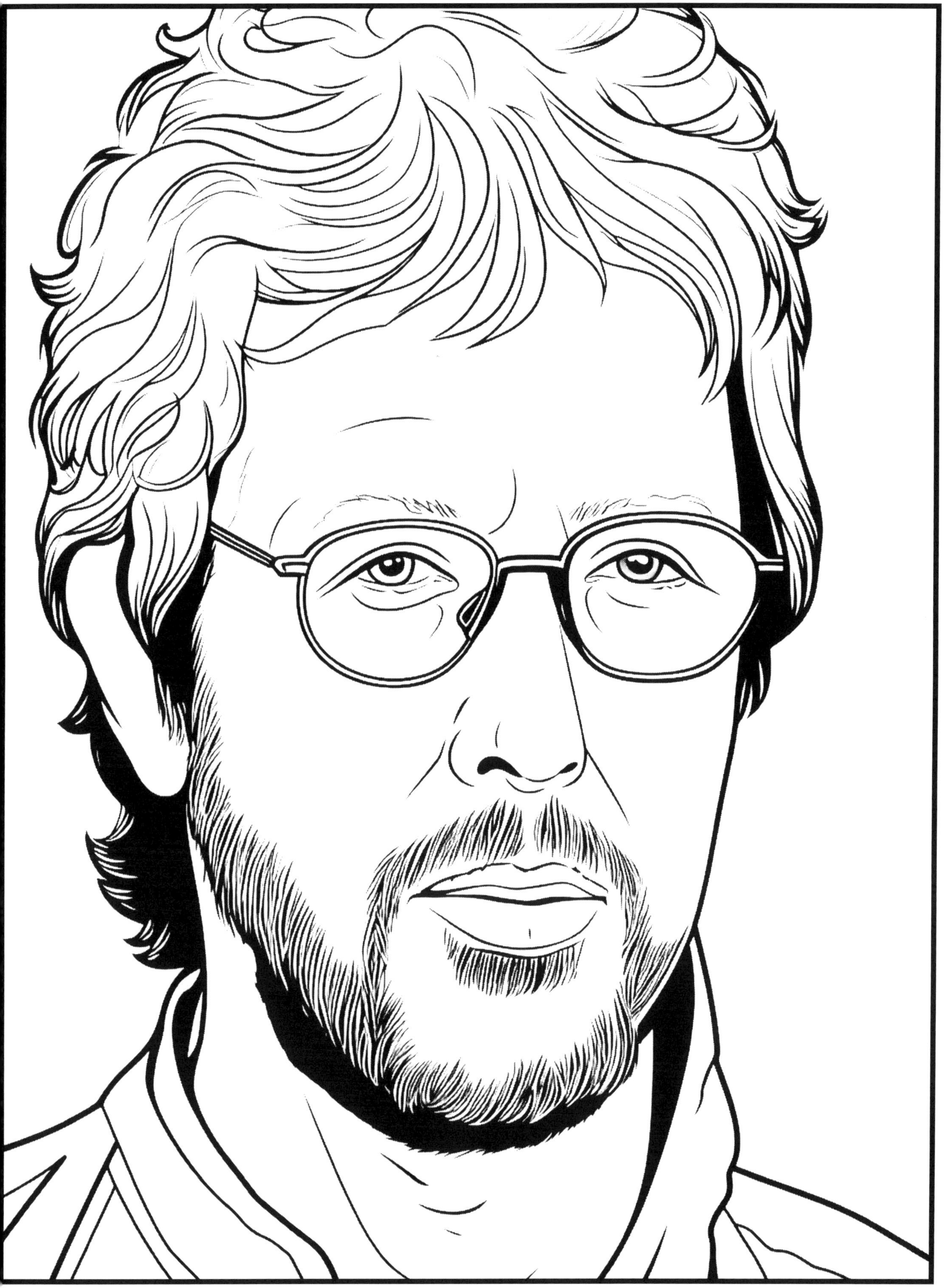

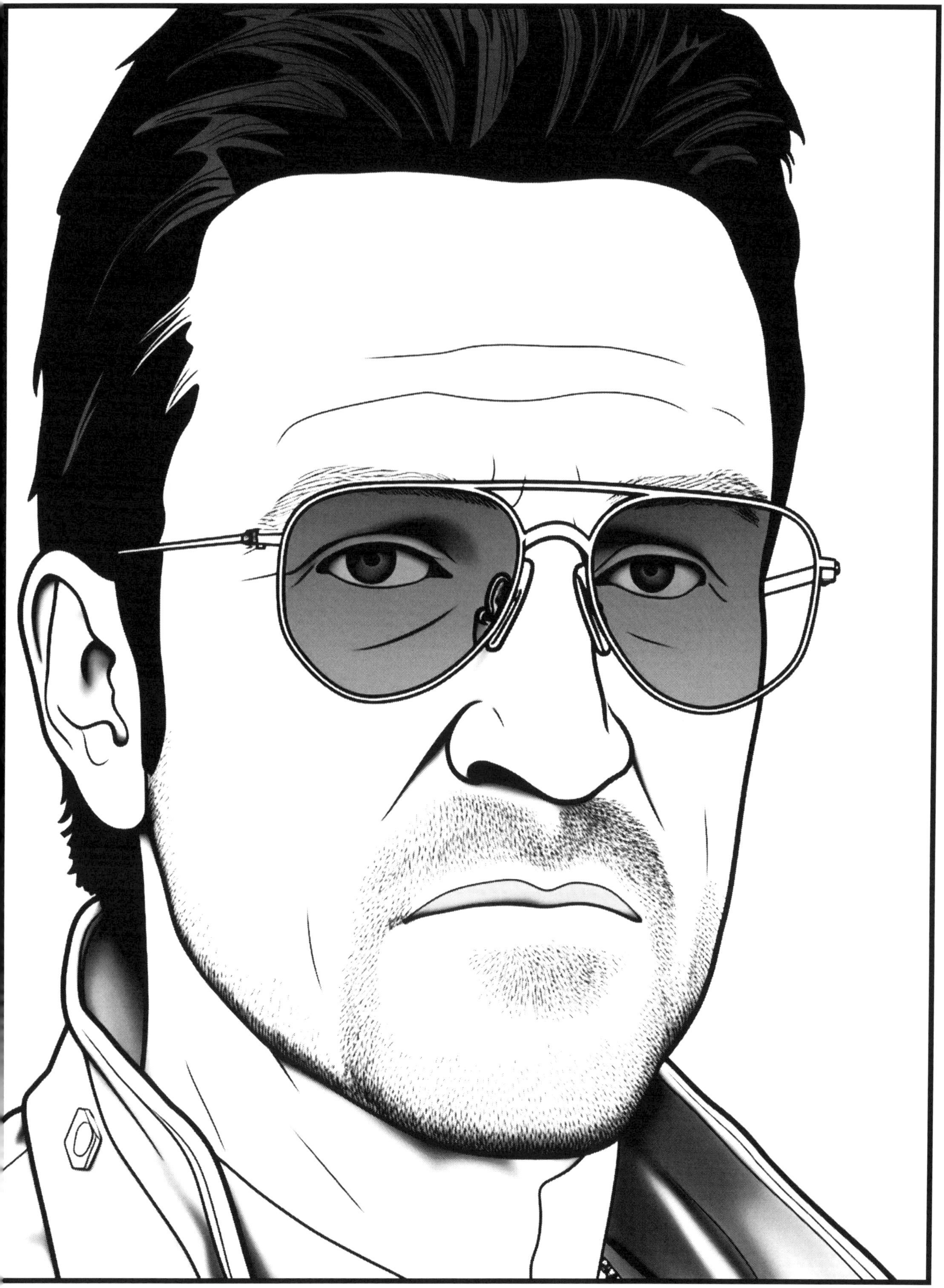

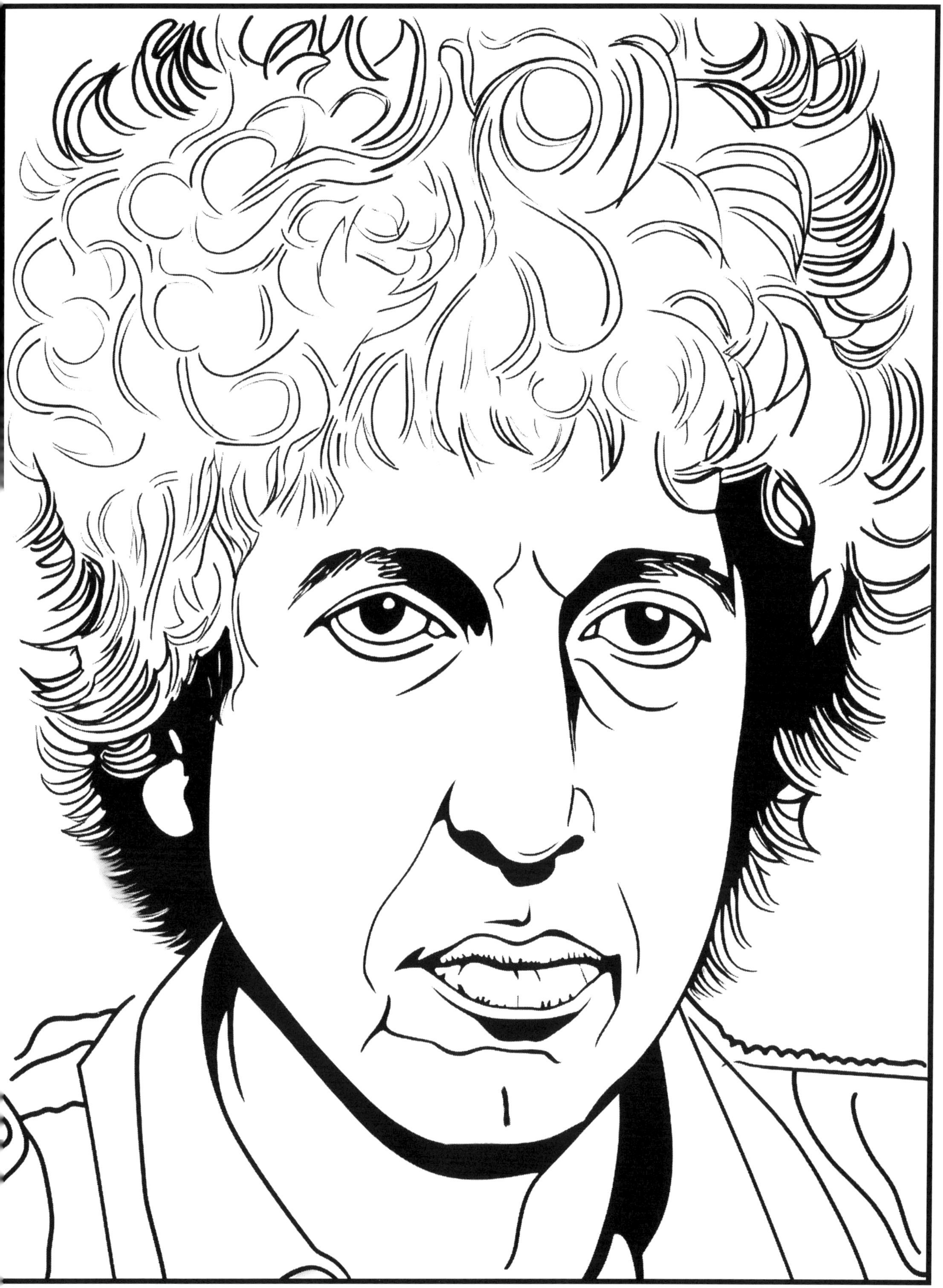

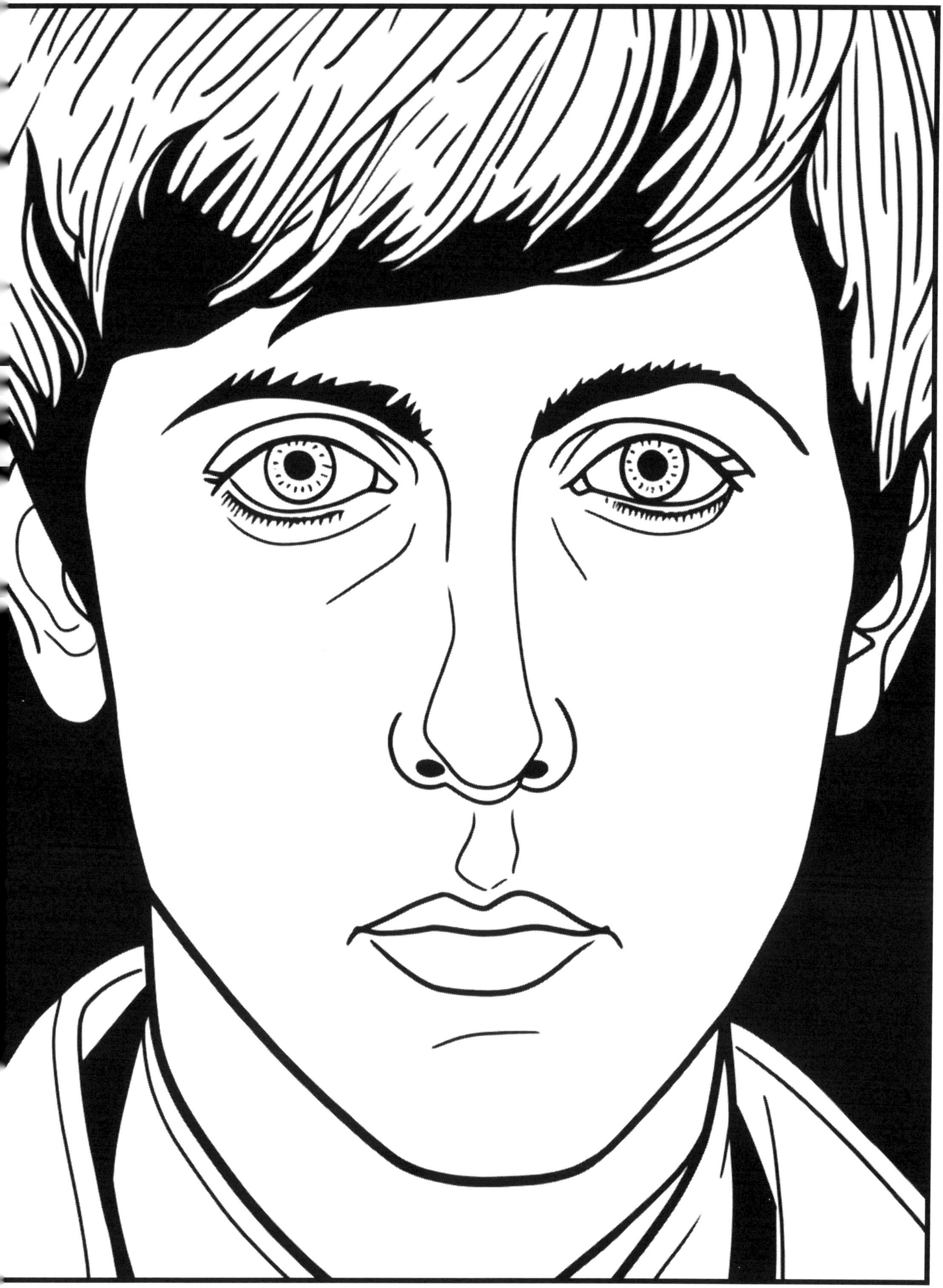

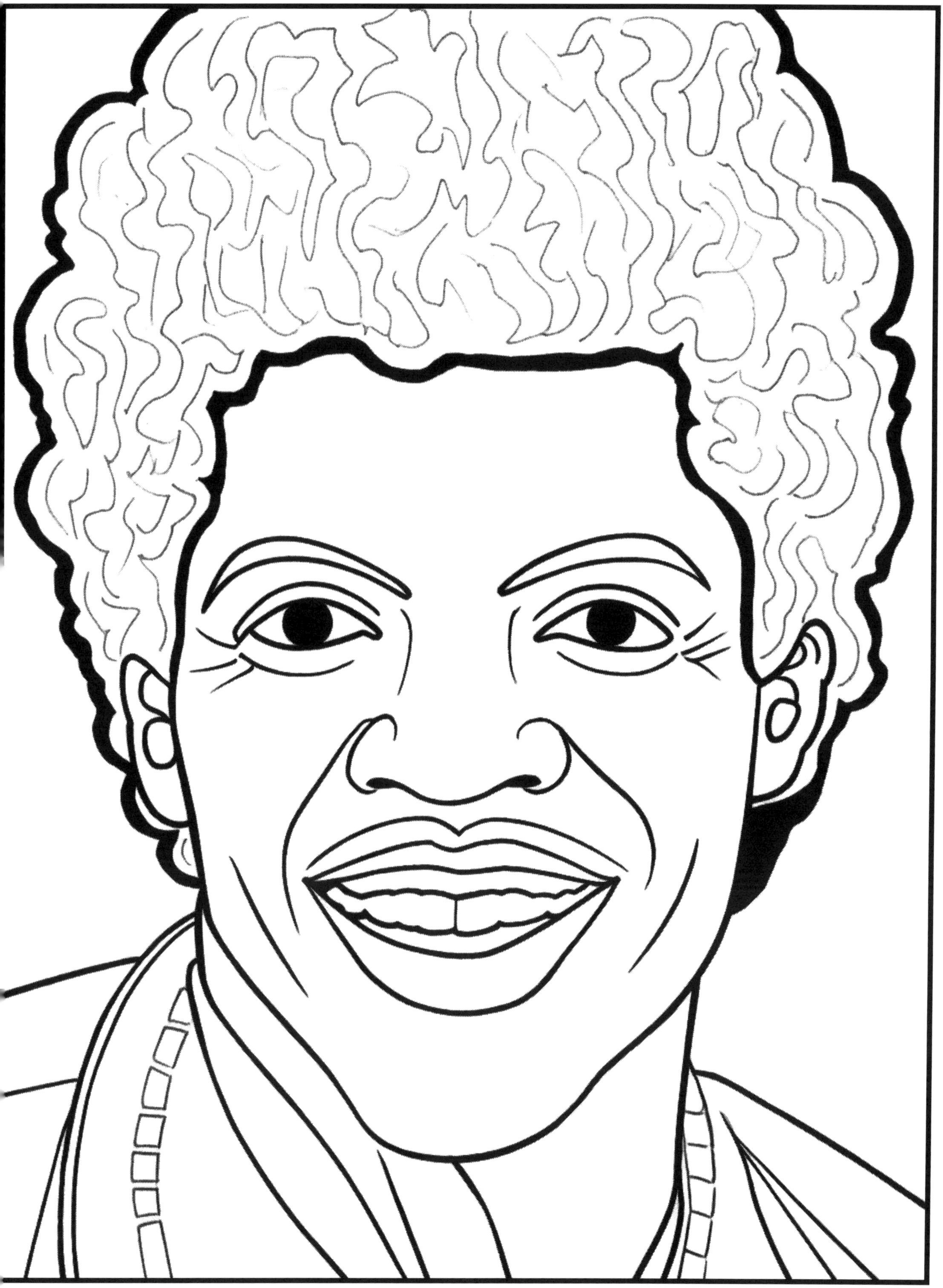

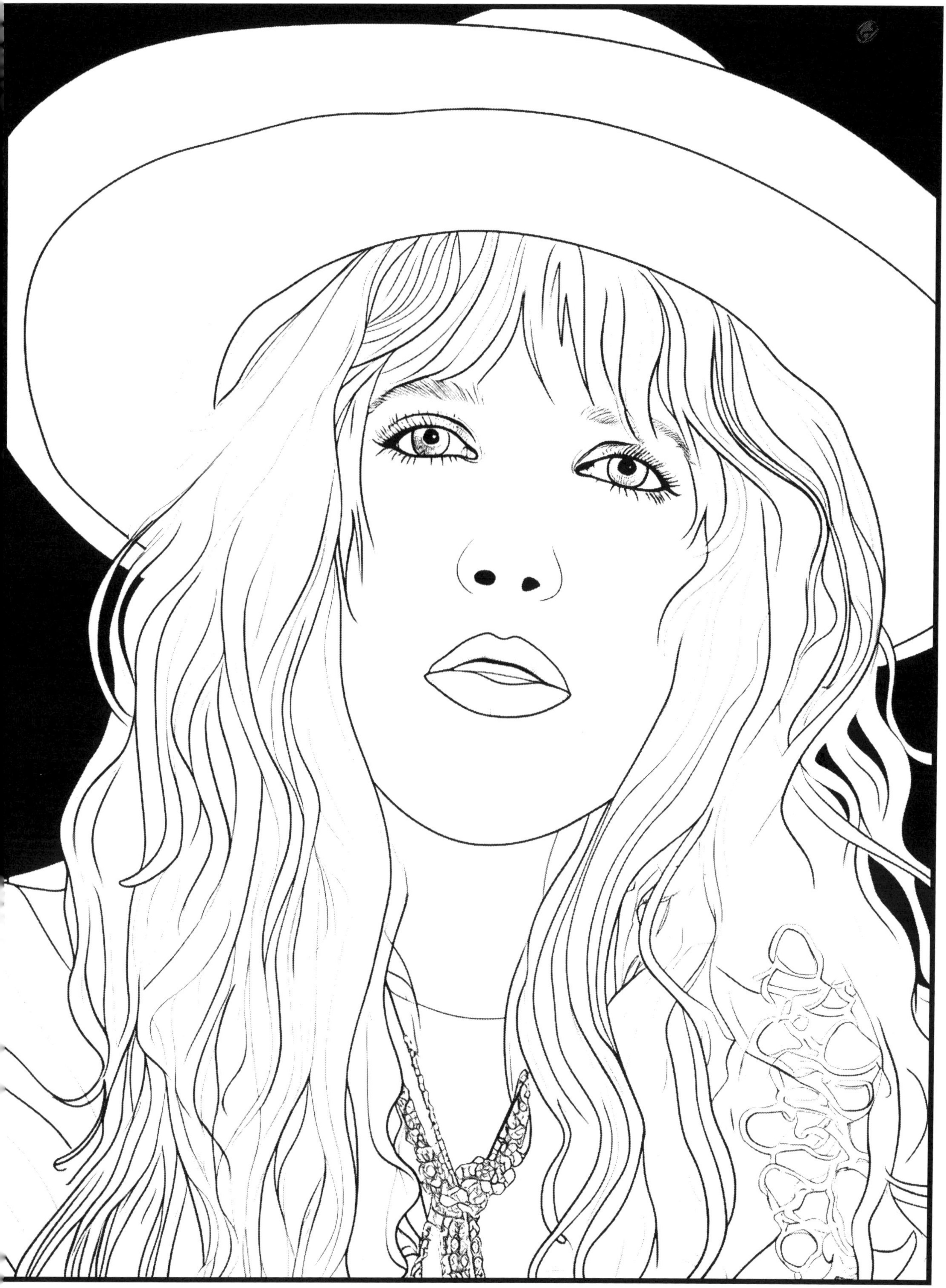

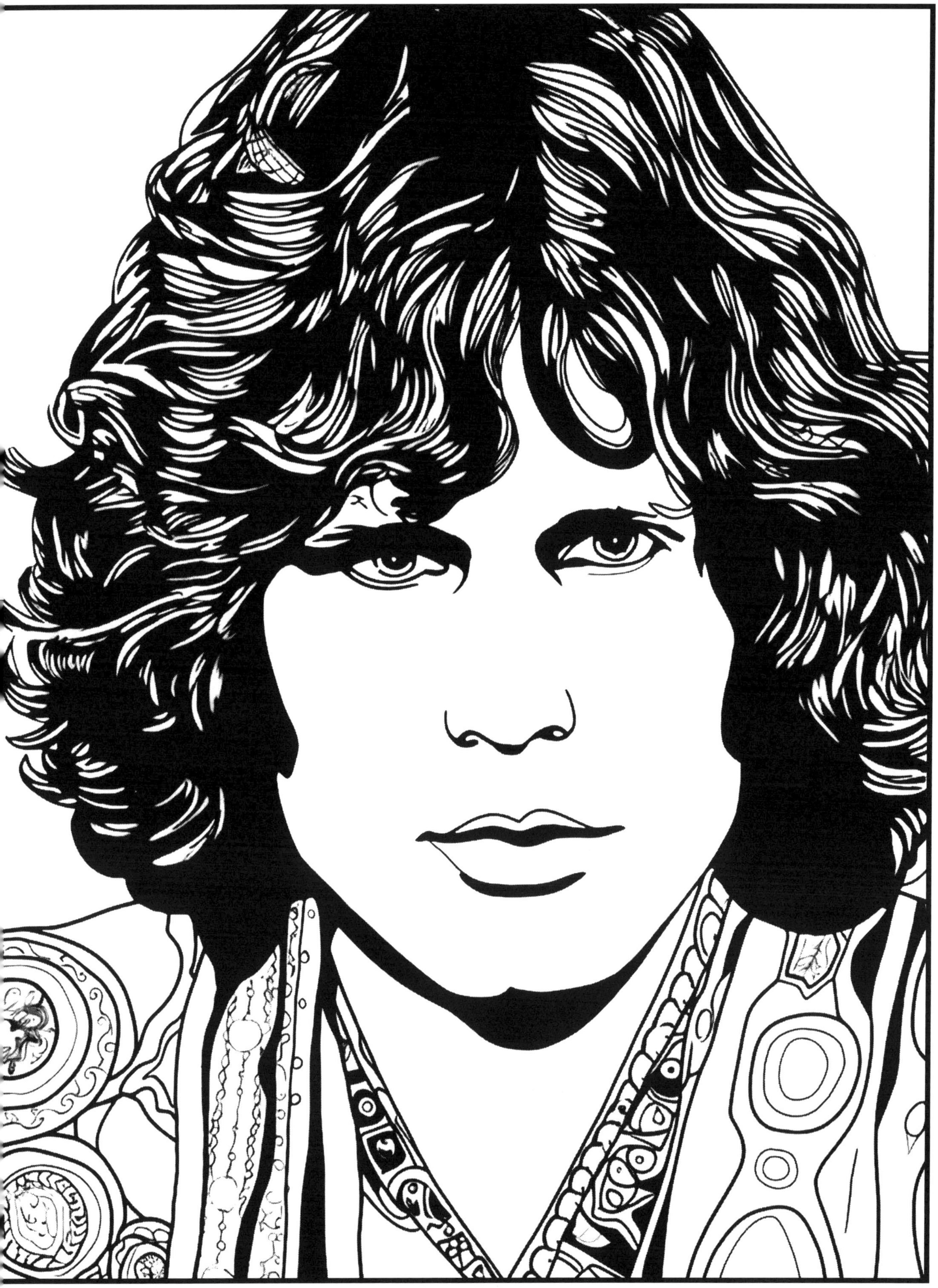

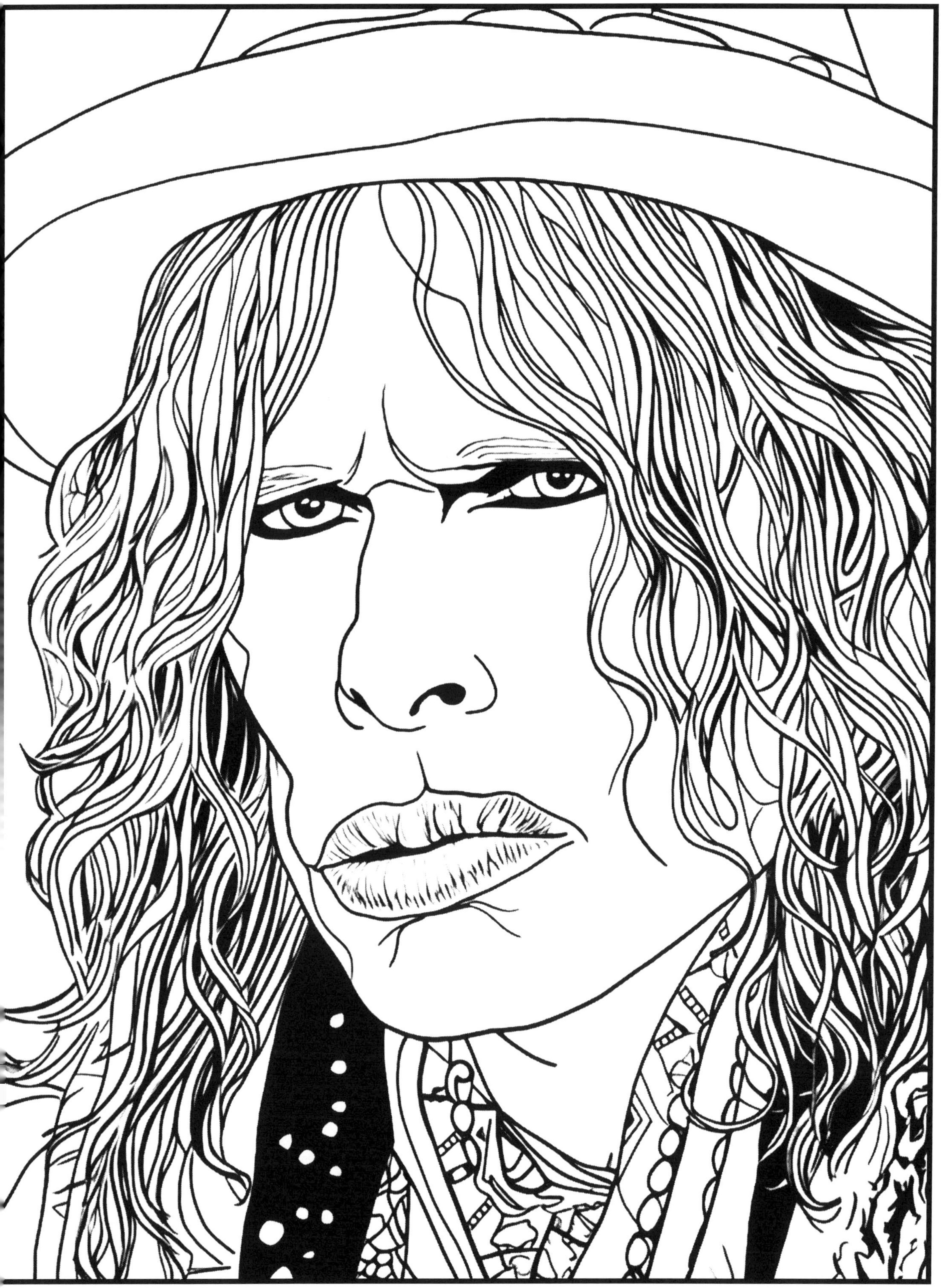

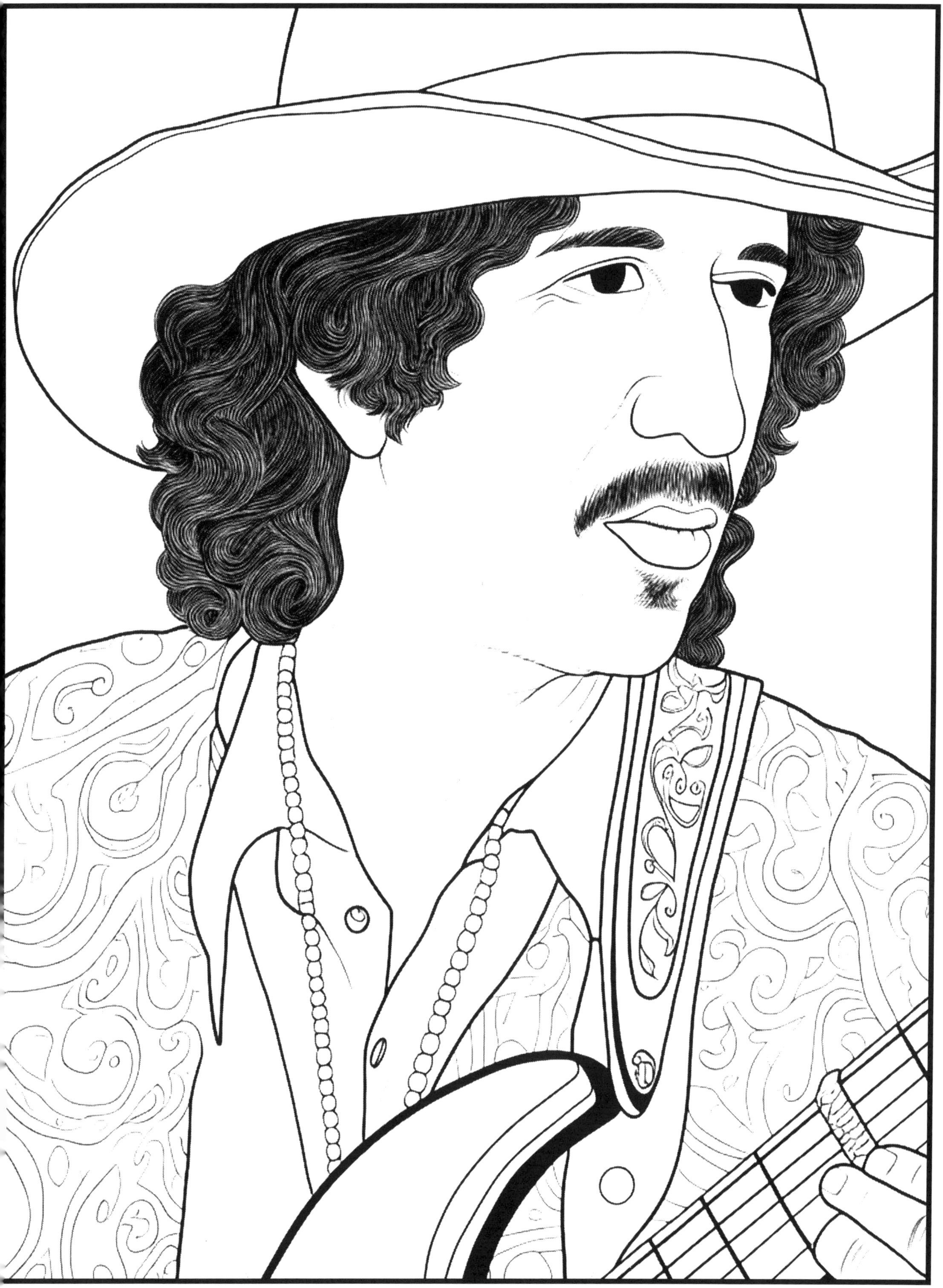

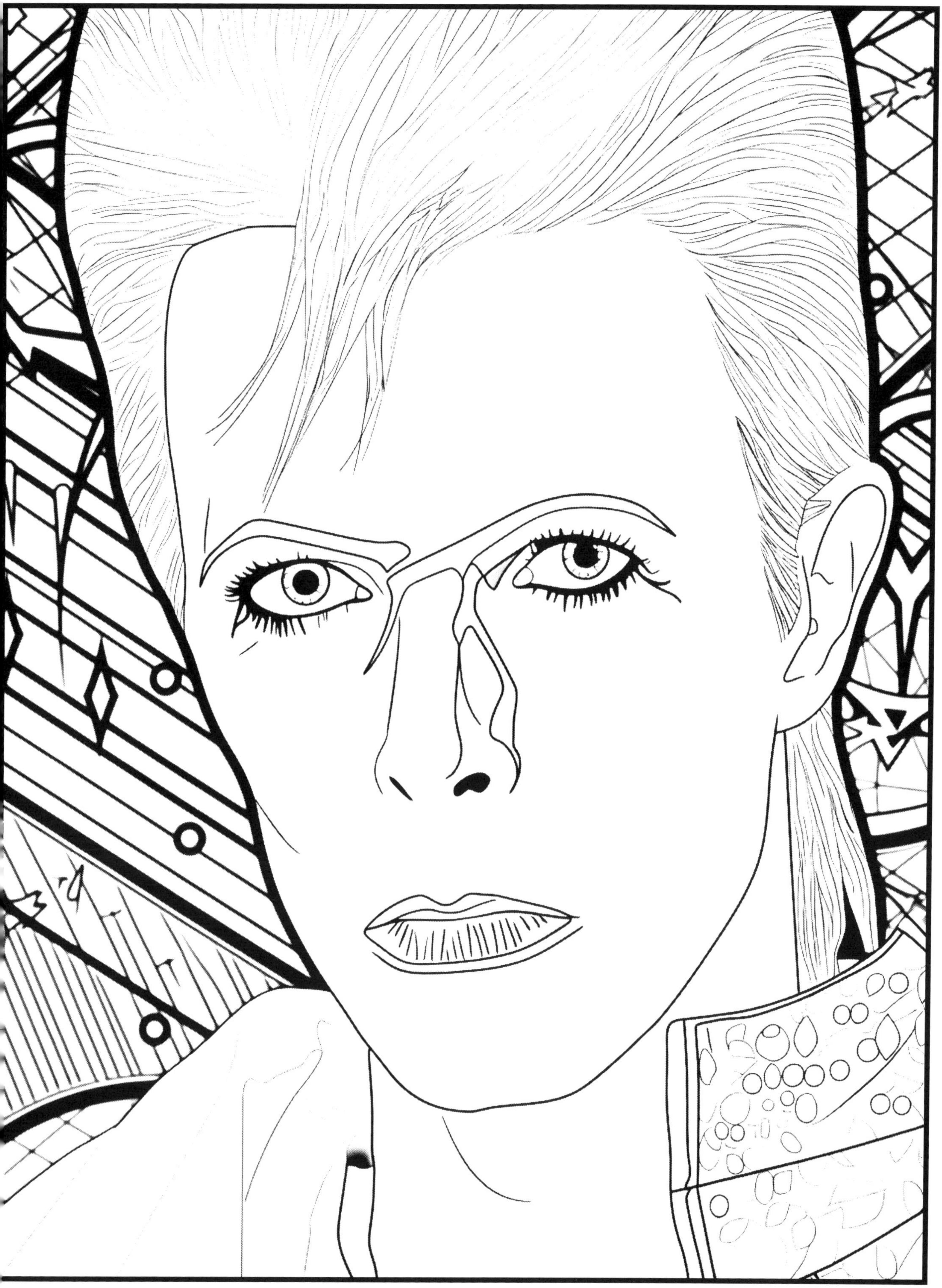

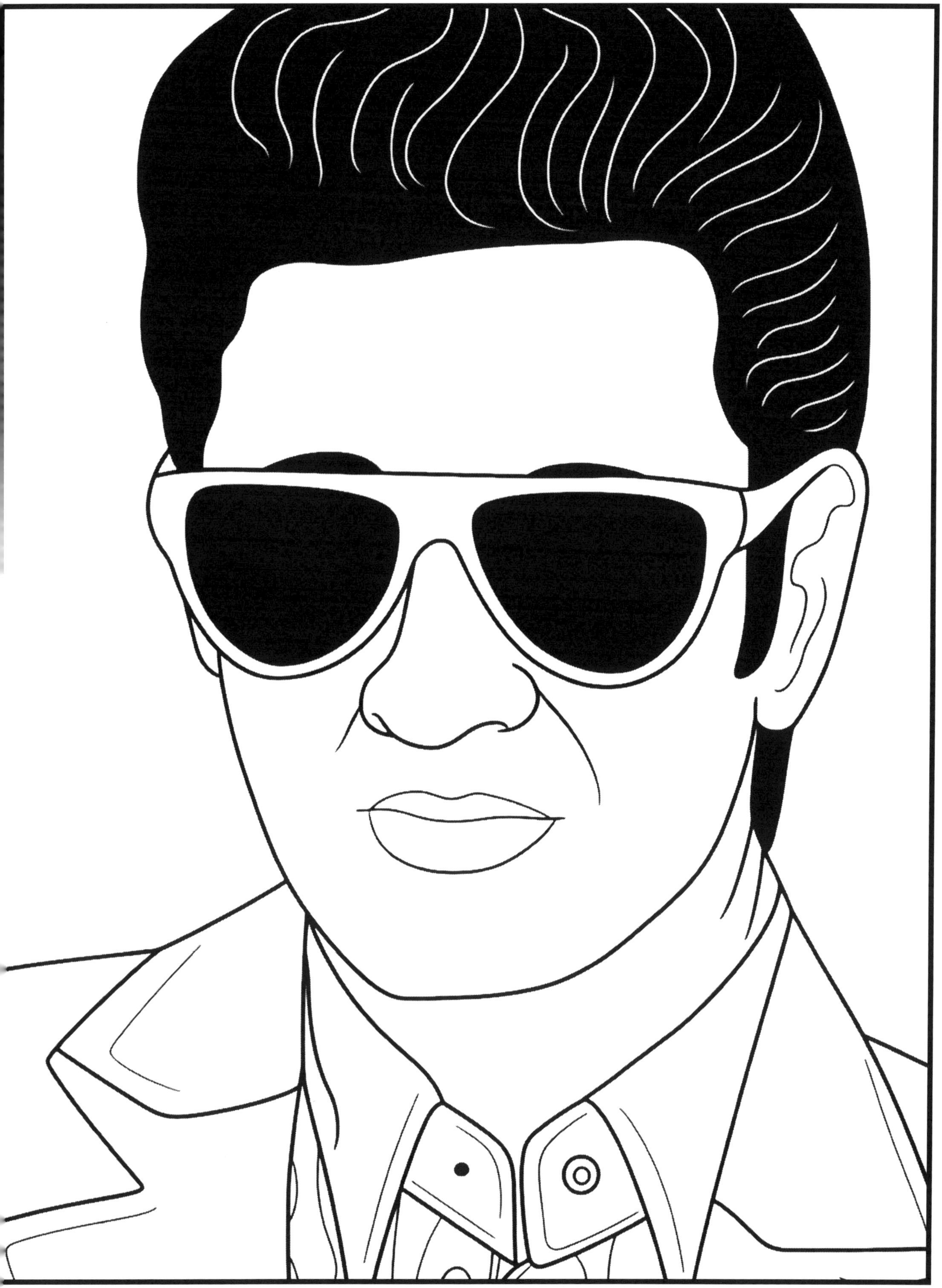

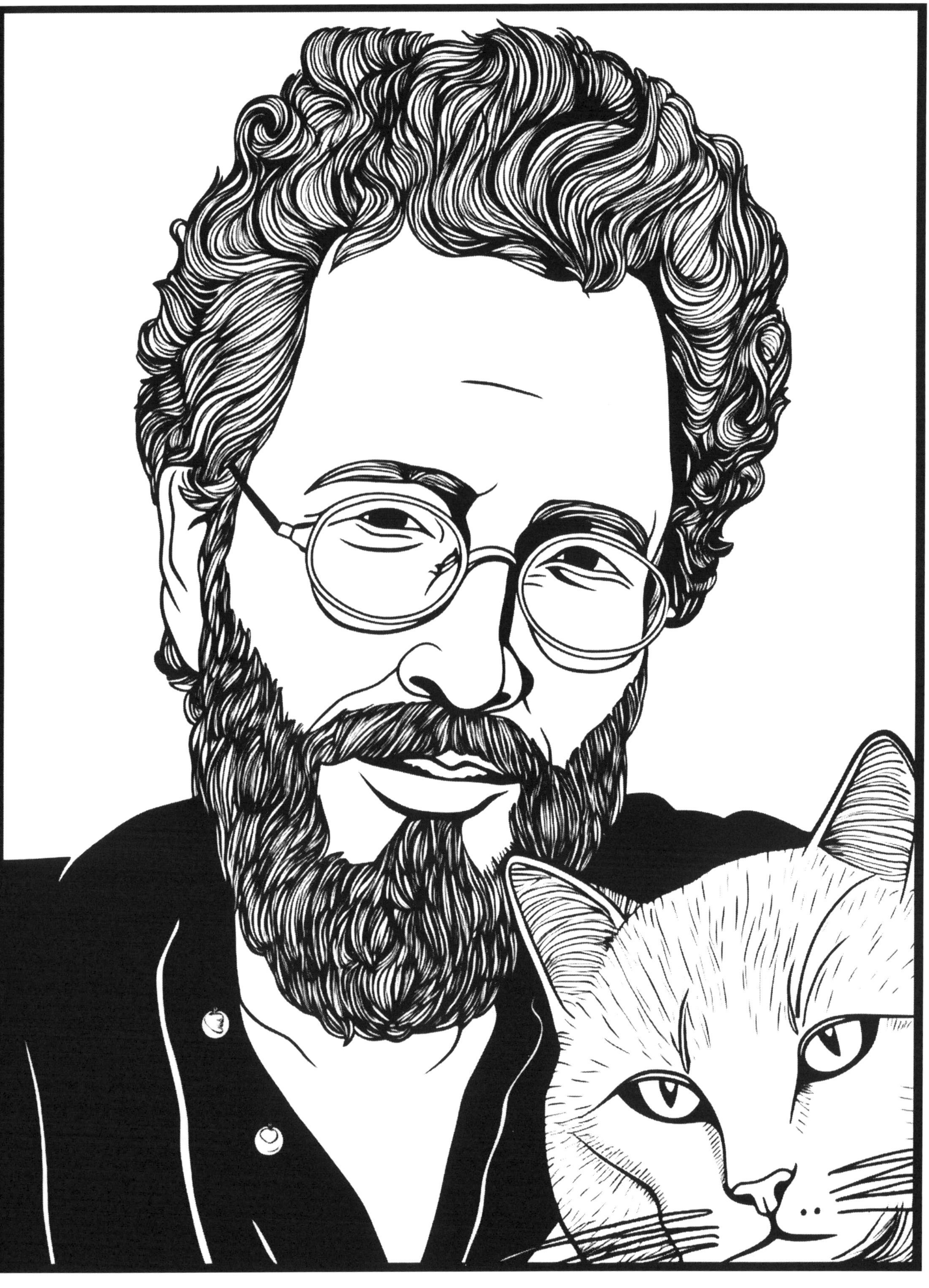

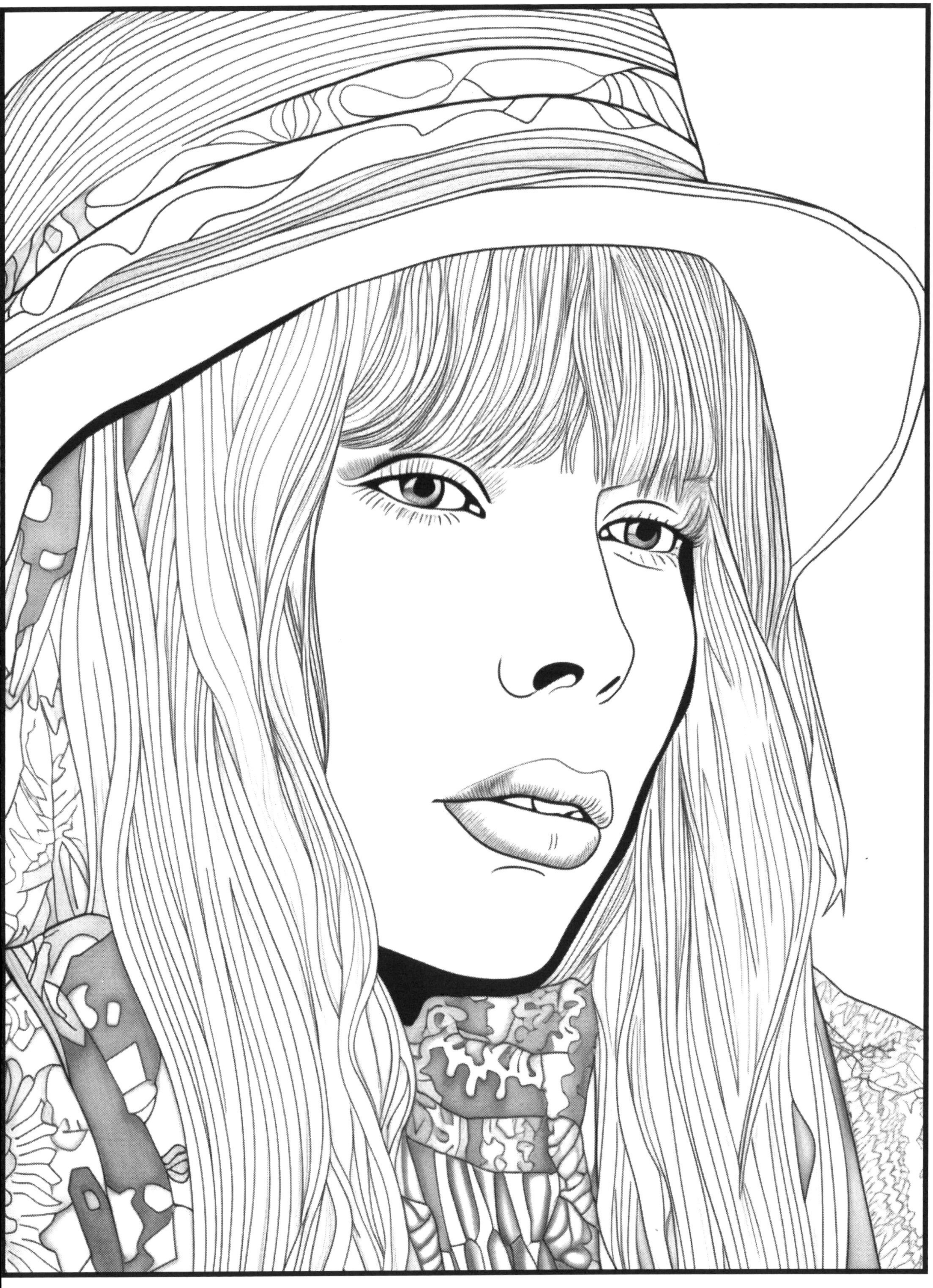

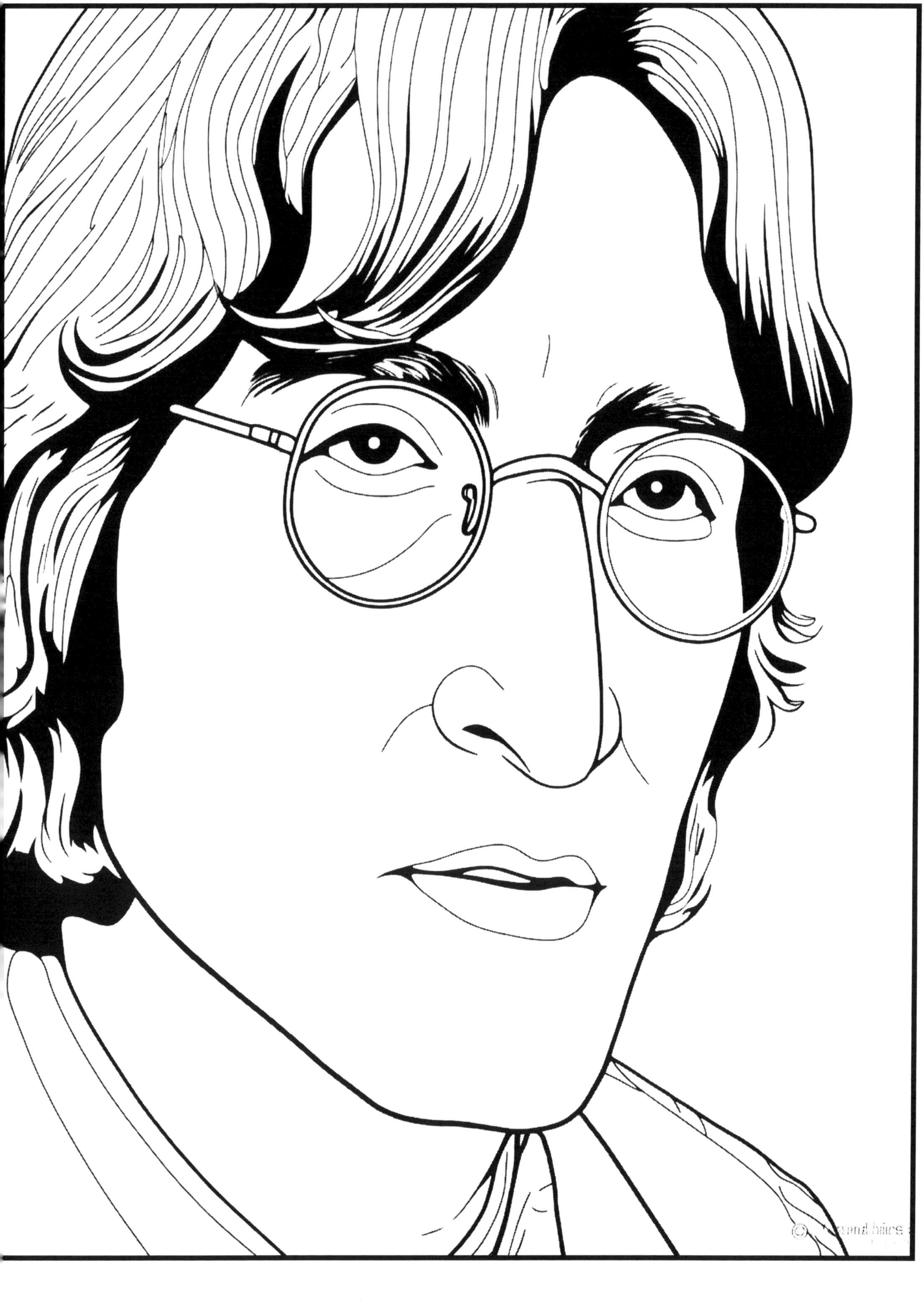

Made in the USA
Las Vegas, NV
02 December 2023

81979050R00052